COMPREHENDING THE GURU
Toward a Grammar of Religious Perception

American Academy of Religion Academy Series

edited by
Carl A. Raschke

Number 57
COMPREHENDING THE GURU
Toward a Grammar of
Religious Perception
by
Daniel Gold

Daniel Gold

COMPREHENDING THE GURU
Toward a Grammar of Religious Perception

Scholars Press
Atlanta, Georgia

COMPREHENDING THE GURU
Toward a Grammar of Religious Perception

by
Daniel Gold

Library of Congress Cataloging-in-Publication Data

Gold, Daniel.
Comprehending the guru.

(American Academy of Religion academy series ; no. 57)
Bibliography: p.
1. Gurus—India. 2. Knowledge, Theory of (Religion)
I. Title. II. Series.
BL2015.G85G65 1987 291.6′1′0954 87-20524
ISBN 1-55540-176-7
ISBN 1-55540-177-5 (pbk.)

Printed in the United States of America
on acid-free paper

TABLE OF CONTENTS

LIST OF FIGURES

PREFACE

Even though historians of religion usually teach that theory can only be known from data, few of us have the patience to read through detailed monographs outside our areas of specialized interest. The present volume aims to resolve this dilemma by organizing the systematic sections of a detailed Indological work around a single extended example. Written several years after the dissertation on which it is based, this version has been greatly shortened, revised to be accessible to the general reader, and framed by some later reflections on the importance of the comparative project it offers. Non-specialists, I am afraid, may still at times find themselves straining to keep Indological details straight; but let them be sustained in their efforts through the author's assurance that, in this book, specific data are given primarily to provide grounding for general religio-historical concepts.

Between the initial conception of the comparative project now presented and the completion of the final manuscript, a number of people have offered comments. Many have no doubt by now forgotten their remarks, sometimes spoken casually, but a few of their words—like the blessings (and curses!) of ancient Indian sages—have ineluctably borne fruit. If those unsuspecting benefactors are surprised at the acknowledgement offered here, I hope it is pleasantly so. Edwin Gerow, early in my studies at the University of Chicago, first revealed the possibility of thinking grammatically about religious materials. Mark Juergensmeyer, who much later read the finished dissertation, made me realize that not all Indologists appreciate this type of thinking, and was the first to suggest that the systematic materials be published separately. A question posed by Bernard Faure after a talk of mine that ended in a happy religious resolution has led to a more unvarnished treatment of the central example offered here: no, religious traditions are not all sweetness and depth. The selection of the example itself had already been influenced by advice from Judith Berling, who wanted to know how the categories she had seen elaborated so systematically could be used to treat an actual problem. Judith also cautioned correctly that putting this book together might be more work than I had initially thought. For practical help and encouragement in persevering with the project, thanks are given to Paul Courtright, Alan Babb, and Carl Raschke.

Thanks have already been offered to my gurus in Chicago and India: *punaḥ punaḥ namaskāra*.

Ithaca, NY D.G.
July, 1987

INTRODUCTION: RELIGIO-HISTORICAL REALITIES

Engrossed in worlds of exuberant myth, ecstatic devotion, and socio-religious drama, historians of religion sometimes have trouble coming to terms with *reality*. The study of religion beckons us with a promise to reveal truths more profoundly real, we presume, than those we might encounter along other disciplinary paths—truths about the depths of the human psyche, about the struggles of man in the world. But the visions of others' reality that we encounter on the way are not always easy for us to take seriously as truth. Certainly, they are often difficult to contemplate more than one at a time: theologies engage in self-conscious argument with one another; different mythologies appear incommensurable.

When feeling generous, we usually manage to understand that all these different claims to truth are somehow relative. They are perspectives, we say, or representations of reality; from a more aesthetic standpoint, they become expressions of the human imagination evoked by genuine problems of life. Having gained a distanced appreciation of the visions found in our materials, we then turn to encompass them within a scholarly understanding. Yet on beginning to explore the scholarly literature we may experience a strange sense of *déja vu:* the multiformity, mutual contradictions, and, perhaps most of all, the disparateness of the realities presented in the data of the world religions are encountered again in the analyses of historians of religion. Should we adopt the same distance to the imaginative constructs of religio-historical analysis as we do to those of the data of religion? Are our realities just as relative as theirs?

There are some reasons to suspect that this is the case. Clear parallels exist between the imagined worlds of the religious subject and the imaginative constructs of the historian of religions. At root, both their visions and our models have common origins: the attempts of human beings to comprehend the universe within their horizon. Moreover, the success of these attempts depends on the perceptiveness with which received, collective traditions of knowledge—religious or academic—are transformed by individual, personally experienced insights. At their best, the constructs of both religious subject and historian of religion reveal an element of intuition that usually emerges only when a person's intellectual vision manages to resonate with his or her genuine existential poise. When worth studying, then, both their classification systems and ours derive from individuals expressing what they honestly sense to be true.

Crucial differences between religious and religio-historical constructs appear, however, in the dynamic between individual and collectively in their creation. Scholarly analyses in the history of religions are most often the creations of persons working by themselves. Their strength lies in the critical perspective of the individual toward a wide array of materials; their insights, in a considered view deriving from an independent vision of reality. For the kinds of truth that these analyses can offer, then, a generous infusion of personal resources is indispensable. Thus, the lack of a monolithic tradition of scholarship in the history of religions is probably necessary for the field's vitality. Nevertheless, the present nearly total lack of coherence does not appear particularly productive. Ambitious attempts at comparison may falter for lack of helpful precedent; with no one taking up the leads of others, pioneering innovations, still incomplete, go nowhere. Too often looking critically at the imaginative constructs of our colleagues with a habit of distance acquired from studying religious texts, each of us begins anew.

By contrast, a good deal of the compelling power of the imagined worlds of religious subjects derives from their naive use of collective traditions. Not the creations of single individuals, they are the products of whole communities sharpening and deepening shared insights. Thus, the diversities that make both our constructs and theirs appear relative have radically different origins. The multiformity of religious subjects' imagined worlds reflects the fullness and complexity of the distinct received traditions in which individual visions take shape; the disparateness of scholars' imaginative constructs, on the other hand, emerges because we take neither our own nor others' work seriously as contributions to a common endeavor.

Perhaps surprisingly to some, the creative benefit of giving credence to the products of a common enterprise has been pointed out by, of all people, Thomas Kuhn. Though remembered primarily for his revelation of the social and cultural factors behind apparently objective scientific truths, Kuhn has also pointed out the creative *power* of a firmly held tradition of scientific knowledge. Not only do most scientists in fact believe in the imaginative constructs that their contemporary science has put before them, but it is their dogged belief in the reality of their models that gives them the determination to pursue unexpected problems to the end.[1] In his headier moments, Kuhn has likened scientists' unquestioned belief in their unseen entities to a religious persuasion,[2] and accordingly, his vision of the social and cultural determinants of the collective tradition of science has long struck a familiar note with historians of religion. Yet it is precisely the parallel between the collective traditions of science and religion that has aroused some of the sharpest indignation of Kuhn's critics, who are intent on demonstrating just how contemporary Western rational knowledge differs from that found in religious traditions, understood by them as archaic and irrational. This felt need to distinguish rational analysis from religious tradition can thus appear as a response to questions similar to those asked by religionists about the reality of their own analyses.

In order to gain enough credence in our own common scholarship to harness the creative power that Kuhn sees generated by adherence to collective traditions, we may then pay attention to some of Kuhn's critics. These critics, working within the bounds of Western epistemology, throw our questions of religious and cultural relativism back onto our own civilization. Instead of comparative religio-historical anxieties about confounding "our" models with "their" myths, a number of recent philosophers of science are pointing out the differences between the realities of *our* specific models, categories, and unseesn entities, and those of *our* all-inclusive myths, metaphysics, and theories.[3]

For the religionist, the crucial distinction drawn by these philosophers is that between global and local realities, between the truths of coherent, infinitely expansible statements about the way the whole of a given environment works, and the objectivity of particular pieces of the picture, finite and at least moderately specific. In the harder sciences, the distinction is sometimes posed as one between realism of theories and of entities: between the reality of, say, the general theory of relativity and that of the unseen entities like electrons or quarks that the theory should be able to comprehend. In the particular humanistic world of the historian of religions, theories seem to correspond to *world-constructions:* the religionist's sense of the whole, which often shows traces of a tradition in which he or she has been immersed—e.g., Eliade's ontology of hierophany and nostalgia, showing clear traces of Hinduism. Entities then correspond to religio-historical constructs: specific academic categories that are taken to religious materials—e.g., Eliade's center of the universe. Analogies between religio-historical constructs and scientific entities suggest some ways in which our types, lists, and formal definitions can be treated as real. These analogies present themselves from two sides: one logical, and the other pragmatic.

Logically, we find strategies of argument that make specific local realities appear independent of grand totalizing visions.[4] In the exact sciences, for example, the same specific mathematical result can sometimes be derived from operations stemming from different hypotheses;[5] when this happens, particular local truths appear to emerge from the intersections of separate global speculations. In this sense, much of the knowledge in physics is overdetermined. When taken to the human sciences, strategies of convergence often rely not on alternative, well-structured theories but on multiple personal perspectives. Thus, distinctions long made in classical Western philosophy suggest that an increase in the number of senses through which we experience an object will reinforce our sense of its reality.[6] We become convinced that the oasis we have begun to discern in the desert is not a mirage when we not only see it, but also smell the trees and feel the coolness of its waters. The same kind of sense perceptions coming from different individuals gives further confirmation: even from afar, we suspect that the oasis is not a hallucination if other people say they see it too. The constructs we in fact find in the human sciences appear less like the totally invisible particles of physics or the vivid hallucinations of the lost and frenzied traveller than like clusters of ponderous but rather ordinary objects at a distance—cultivated, well-kept trees marking an overgrown landscape; a group of sculptures arranged in a park. Indistinct at first and imperfect, their outlines become clearer as we get closer to them and see them in their context. Then, if others say they see them too, we grow confident that they are not hallucinations.

Another level of conviction is reached when we are able to touch (if not smell) them, and then find them substantial enough to manipulate. At this point, we may start doing our own work on the sculptures, altering them and shifting their positions better to show off their contexts; or we take shoots from the trees to plant them in a different configuration and tend them in our own personal style: perhaps these will be the stronger growths, which flourish. Thus, though many of us may be able to discern the outlines of the same object when it is pointed out, on closer examination each of us is likely to see it differently and handle it in his or her own way. The logic of convergence, then, is followed by the pragmatics of experiment, and the persuasive and creative force of both grows with collectivity: the more our constructs are seen and used, the more they actually seem to be there and grow. What at the moment is lacking in history of religions is a critical mass of seriously held constructs around which a collectivity can form.

In history of religions, a logic of convergence emerges naturally from the constitution of the discipline. For the substantial reality of constructs will be confirmed by the genuine multiplicity of perspectives that must converge on them. The problem with strategies of argument through convergence, proponents admit, is that shared theories are likely to result in common perceptions; so scholars working within homogeneous communities must be careful to make sure that individual perspectives really are different, disentangling specific perception from larger theories.[7] This is less of a problem in history of religions, at least as it is now constituted, than in many other traditions of scholarship. For while we may share some common approaches, our individual world-constructions reveal an immense diversity—a diversity that derives not only from an experience, however vicarious, of the religions that we study, but also from a related ambivalence toward our own natal traditions. Our world-constructions, articulate or not, are usually orthodox by no one's standards, and are sometimes highly idiosyncratic. So when the world-constructions of a number of historians of religion do converge, it is usually worth taking a serious look at the place of intersection. Moreover, constructs becoming common property in history of religions will have to be able to support different traditional world-constructions that are historically and geographically distinct. Typologies, formalized concepts, and morphological frames that can withstand pressure from so many different directions—we eventually have reason to believe—perhaps really do correspond to some natural categories. Thus, the same diverse views that make total theoretical agreement inconceivable among historians of religion can, in their convergence, help establish partial truths.

The payoff in any field, however, emerges from the pragmatics of experiment. And, unfortunately, most of the constructs that we establish we do not use effectively. The story that Ian Hacking tells of how he first started thinking about the reality of entities also suggests the creative power to which belief in that reality can lead. Hacking heard of an experiment in which admittedly invisible electrons were being sprayed onto niobium balls in order to investigate even more invisible quarks. It was not the quarks that convinced him of the reality of entities, but the electrons: as far as Hacking was concerned, "if you can spray them, then they are real."[8] Thus, a mark of an object's evident reality is its potential to be used for further discovery. The phenomenology of religions, in its different forms, has known no dearth of categories, but these have too often been taken as ends in themselves. Even Eliade's constructs—revitalizing history of religions through their depth and scope—never managed to pass beyond a state of becoming established, traced out again and again in different contexts. Exhausted through their long process of establishment, they have not seriously been used to pursue problems beyond themselves, and their vitality in the past decades has waned. Though Eliade's followers may have, in their enthusiasm, sprayed centers of the universe onto religious worlds, they did not usually do so to go after new, religio-historical quarks. Trusting in our concepts, we must take them one step further and manipulate them more deliberately to solve problems of religious materials.

For it is in the problems that history of religions treats that its attraction lies. Constructs solid enough to withstand the varied scrutiny and use to which they can collectively be put are likely to be dull and fairly compact. Simpler than the connected concepts emerging from Eliade's eminently articulate world-vision, they emerge individually as types ("holy man"), definitions ("Hinduism")[9], and broadly conceived processes ("routinization"). Whatever degree of reality we give to these concepts, they are, in themselves, most unexciting. Their interest derives from the problems with which they can deal: outward dynamics of tradition (authority, community, adaptation); tensions of inner life (moral choice, disciplined practice, mystical vision); and, perhaps most intriguing, the complex relationships between outer tradition and inner life.

Our problem as historians of religion is to understand problems of human beings struggling to comprehend their existence in the world. Our religio-historical constructs must then be able to make sense of the worlds that they conceive. The realities of their worlds and our constructs have different potencies. The worlds of religious subjects reveal powerful existential truths; but these too often remain distant from us, apparently beyond our grasp. Our constructs—themselves lifeless—attain familiar, graspable objectivity as they are seen and used; but they appear vital only when they serve as handles on the religious worlds of others.

Where do we look for these religious worlds? Unlike electrons and quarks, religio-historical constructs are not usually supposed to correspond exactly to realities of the outside world: religious man, we have been told, can find centers of the universe everywhere. Yet if the centers of the universe that religious individuals perceive were solely in their imaginations, we would not be able to perceive them at all. The realities we attempt to grasp lie somewhere between the inside and the outside, in the relationship between the ways in which religious individuals comprehend the world and the situations that the world deals them.

This movement between outer and inner is reflected in our own work as we shift from outwardly known specifics to more inwardly conceived generalizations, back and forth, refining our constructs as we use them. The specifics exist not only on the mythic and existential level pointed out by Eliade, but also in the social and cultural spheres treated by Weber and Geertz. The generalizations start from our own idiosyncratic world-constructions, and our constructs reflect the realities of religious perception that we are able to conceive. These can more accurately reflect the realities that we penetrate by being shared and tested, in this way being transformed from individually conceived insights into common starting points for inquiry. Thus grappling with each others' constructs, we may be able to grow and give shape to a body of collective knowledge about the human religious imagination—its capacities, limits, and general inclinations; its modes of interaction with specific cultural institutions and historical events.

What is the status of this religio-historical knowledge? Is it, finally, as relative as the knowledge of religious subjects on which it reflects? To the extent that it strives to be global, like religious knowledge, probably so. But religious and religio-historical knowledge are relative in different ways. Religious knowledge, sympathetically considered, offers a partial vision of the whole, a vision that grows deeper as it moves steadily in one direction. Religio-historical knowledge, by contrast, is one of linked pieces and changing perspectives, moving from very shallow to moderately deep and back again—and sometimes, as it spreads out, offering us a glimpse of symmetrical wholeness in temporary balance. The firmness of religio-historical knowledge is in its links: in the points at which different perspectives intersect, in the nodes at which data from diverse traditions manage to connect with each other. This book attempts to present some nodes around which religio-historical knowledge might converge.

Though here directed widely outward in a spirit of comparative adventure, the constructs to be described have their origins in the study of one tradition, with some distinctive problems of its own. The tradition is that of the sants of North India, and the problems derive from the mystery of the guru that the sants present. Sants are remembered in North India from the beginning of the fifteenth century, a time when Islam had made its impact felt as a political and cultural force, but before the synthetic Indo-Muslim culture had taken shape under the Mughals. Two of the most influential early sants—Kabīr and Dādū—seem to have come from low Hindu castes recently converted to Islam, and sang in their Hindi vernaculars of a Lord who transcended the orthodoxies of both traditions. The North Indian sants have predecessors in earlier traditions to the South, but are distinguished from most of those through a devotion that is characteristically aniconic. Thus, the sants' piety is known to scholars of Hindi as *nirguṇ bhakti*, devotion to the Formless Lord. Kabīr, in fact, as well as some other sants knew a devotion not only aniconic but frankly iconoclastic, exalting the Formless, Transcendent Lord at the expense of the great gods of India and the rituals of Hinduism and Islam. The sants often sang instead of the guru, or the "true guru"—terms that sometimes seem to refer to the Lord above but also frequently suggest a living holy man. At any rate, to the extent that the sants existed as a tradition at all, they were clearly a tradition of holy men, with no fixed scriptures or set institutional forms. Idiosyncratic, making their own syntheses, each of the well-known sants recreated their tradition from the resources they knew. At the same time, however, they explicitly recognized each other as brethren—later sants, for example, citing earlier ones in songs. Thus, perhaps the most perplexing general question arising from a study of the sants is why this group of idiosyncratic individuals cherished the idea of a tradition at all.

The origins of this book lie in an attempt to answer that question through an examination of the sants as a tradition of holy men—a study contrasting the holy man as object of faith to comparable objects found in the history of religions. Of these, two main types have emerged: great gods and founders, existing once and for all; and the concept of tradition itself, exemplified in India in the eternal Vedic heritage. These bases of faith for the believer then turn into the bases of formalized constructs for the historian of religions. Simple categories themselves, their interest lies in the relationships that they can reveal among factors of religious life and institutions, and what they suggest about the propensities of the human imagination. For religious life, the holy man, singular personality of the god, and eternal heritage of tradition appear to be hierophanies, as Eliade might say, with their own distinctive ways of presenting the divine. For institutions, they signal various stages in a Weberian process of routinization of charisma. Moreover, when the abstract relationships they form among themselves are traced out over a broad comparative context, they seem to indicate some limits of human religious perception. Presenting a morphology of problems found in religious materials and some abstract patterns of syntax among themselves, these constructs become the elements of a grammar of religious perception.

In a separate book, written for Indologists, I used this grammar to examine the sants in their complex Indian environment, focusing on their synthetic origins.[10] Here I would like to develop the comparative dimensions of the grammar for general historians of religions. The sants still provide the basis for the presentation, but the Indic materials have here been greatly condensed, subordinated to methodological concerns. Chapter 1 uses the situation of an important eighteenth-century sant named Palṭū to elaborate the basic categories at length, and in so doing identifies some distinctive problems of the sants as a tradition of holy men. Chapter 2, highlighting the categories' morphological dimensions, uses them to analyze a contemporary crisis in Palṭū's extended lineage. Chapter 3 turns to the syntax, and through broad abstract comparisons suggests an answer to the perplexing problem of the *idea* of sant tradition. Chapter 4 then examines the potentials of the grammar as an instrument of general religio-historical knowledge, using it to try to understand the role of sants and other Indian gurus in the West today.

An epilogue, finally, reconsiders our initial questions about the relationships between religious and religio-historical knowledge by reflecting on some ways in which sants and historians of religion deal as individuals with their respective traditions. As individuals, both sants and religionists often appear highly idiosyncratic, while the cumulative traditions faced by both are just as highly diffuse. Given this parallel between our situation and theirs, an understanding of our own institutions might be enhanced by paying attention to those of the sants. Clearly, the realities of immediate concern to sants and religionists are of different orders—most sants, I suspect, would mock our endeavor as empty pedantry. Thus, the religionist's attempt to combine a sympathy for the realities of which the sants sang with a serious attention to academic constructs appears as a violent bringing together of opposites. But this attempt is nonetheless essential to our task. Already there appears a striking similarity between us and them: the history of religions, like religion itself, is grounded in paradox.

NOTES

/1/ See "The Essential Tension: Tradition and Innovation in Scientific Research" in Kuhn's *The Essential Tension: Selected Studies in Scientific Tradition and Change* (Chicago: University of Chicago Press, 1977). The essay was first published in 1959, three years before Kuhn's classic *The Structure of Scientific Revolutions* (Chicago: University of Chicago Press, 1962), pp. 223–239.

/2/ Some passages in *Structure of Scientific Revolutions* where Kuhn likens science to theology are pointed out by J. W. N. Watkins in "Against Normal Science" (*Criticism and the Growth of Knowledge*, ed. Imre Lakatos and Alan Musgrave [London: Cambridge University Press, 1970], pp. 25–37).

/3/ Brian Ellis (*Rational Belief Systems* [Totowa, New Jersey. Rowman and Littlefield, 1979], p. 28, f 15) may have been the first to articulate a "scientific-entity realism" as a position in the philosophy of science. A version of this position is elaborated neatly for the layman by Ian Hacking in *Representing and Intervening: Introductory Topics in the Philosophy of Natural Science* (Cambridge: Cambridge University Press, 1983). In *How the Laws of Physics Lie* (Oxford: Clarendon Press, 1982), pp. 87–99, Nancy Cartwright relates the position to current empirical approaches. For explicit comparisons of post-Kuhnian realism in philosophy and theology see Arthur Peacock, *Intimations of Reality: Critical Realism in Science and Religion* (Notre Dame, Indiana: University of Notre Dame Press, 1984).

/4/Practical work on these strategies was pioneered by Donald T. Campbell, who called his approach "descriptive epistemology." An excellent introduction to Campbell's approach together with a bibliography of his works is offered by *Scientific Inquiry and the Social Sciences: A Volume in Honor of Donald T. Campbell*, ed. Marilynn B. Brewer and Barry E. Collins (San Francisco: Jossey-Bass Publishers, 1981).

/5/ Richard P. Feynman gives an easily understandable example of this phenomenon in his popular volume *The Character of Physical Law* (Cambridge, Mass: M.I.T. Press, 1965), pp. 49–53.
/6/ In his valuable "Robustness, Reliability, and Overdetermination," (in Brewer and Collins, *Scientific Inquiry*, pp. 124–163), William C. Wimsatt suggests some implications of the distinction between primary and secondary qualities known to Galileo, Descartes, and Locke: "Primary qualities—such as shape, figure, and size—are detectable in more than one sensory modality. Secondary qualities—such as color, taste, and sound—are detectable through only one sense" (p. 146).
/7/ See Marilynn B. Brewer and Barry E. Collins, "Perspectives on Knowing: Six Themes from Donald T. Campbell" (Introduction to their *Scientific Inquiry*, pp. 1–9).
/8/ Hacking, *Representing and Intervening*, pp. 22–23.
/9/ For reflections on problems of definition in Hindu studies see Brian K. Smith, "Exorcising the Transcendent: Strategies for Defining Hinduism and Religion," *History of Religions* 27: 32–55.
/10/ *The Lord as Guru: Hindi Sants in North Indian Tradition* (New York: Oxford University Press, 1987).

CHAPTER 1

PRESENTING THE FOCI: PALṬŪ IN AYODHYĀ

Not every devotee settled in Rām's ancient capital at Ayodhyā has venerated Rām as Lord. Today, pilgrims come to Ayodhyā from all over India to bathe in the waters of the river Saryū and adore the images of Rām displayed throughout the town. But Palṭū Sāhib, an eighteenth-century devotee who had come to Ayodhyā from an outlying village, found little value in ritual baths and prostrations to Rām's image. His verses instead proclaim the glory of a Formless Lord, existing apart from the captivating images that inhabit Hindu shrines. Not attracted to the Lord as a mythic personality, Palṭū experienced the divine in more subtle ways. He rose up to "the eighth of the heavens" and heard "sounds coming down from the sky." Steadily, "like a stream of oil," Palṭū drew his consciousness within.[1] For Palṭū had learned yogic secrets from a guru named Govind, who, they say, learned them from his guru Bhīkhā, who stood in turn within an important lineage of Hindi sants.

The guru whom the sants worship is a mysterious being. Palṭū sings of the guru in the same language he uses to describe his experience of the highest divine: the guru, like heavenly sound, "comes down from the sky"; and it is the guru, Palṭū affirms, who sometimes draws him within.[2] The guru thus often appears as an incorporeal divinity, indeed, sometimes as the Formless Lord himself. Yet at the same time, the living guru—at once the authoritative teacher demanded by yoga as well as the primary focus available for devotion—can loom large indeed in the eyes of his disciple. Palṭū, then, sometimes portrays the guru he contemplates inwardly in distinctly human terms. Without the guru, Palṭū tell us, ascetic practice will be fruitless, not to mention pilgrimage to places like Ayodhyā, Kāśī, and Prayāg. Only through single-minded devotion to the guru will the disciple be sure to come out ahead:

I'll give up all the rest to contemplate the guru. [Refrain]

I won't worship Brahma, Visṇu, or Maheśa,
  Nor fix attention on a god of stone.
The object of my love resides within my body;
  To him alone I'll bow my head. (1)
I won't worship Brahma, Viṣṇu, or Maheśa,
  Or take the pilgrim's walk around the town.
Should I reach Prayāg, I won't go to the bathing place,
  Nor will I sacrifice myself to Jagannāth at Purī. (2)
Sādhū, I won't mutter wordless phrases
  Or fix my gaze between my eyes.
Nor will I stretch to sit in yogic posture
  And play myself internal sounds. (3)
Sādhū, I'll abandon all God's names
  To take the one my guru gave.
The guru's image overspreads my heart
  And gets all my attention. (4)
When he obliterates our separateness
  What's left I'll call the Formless.
The world within the sky will be our Kingdom
  And with fanfare I will call out, "I am He." (5)
At my turn in the game of love, says Palṭū,
  I'll gamble with the guru.
I get the guru if I win, and if I lose
  I still will say I'm his. (6)[3]

Although Palṭū's ardent guru-devotion was experienced by many sants, his strident iconoclasm was more characteristically his own. The sants were a highly diverse group, coming from different regional and socio-religious backgrounds and displaying distinctive personal styles. In a heterogeneous India that knew Islamic ways as well as Hindu ones, they carry on the role of the individualistic holy man that took shape in an earlier tantric era. Beholden only to their gurus and caring little for convention, some, like Palṭū, revelled in bombastic barbs. Others presented original hybrids more accommodating to the various Hindu and Muslim traditions around them.

The sants most formative to the tradition grew up beyond the range of established orthodoxies. Two of the most important—Kabīr and Dādū—were born in Hindu castes recently converted to Islam, and the earliest sants came largely from the lowest strata of Hindu society. Yet though the Formless Lord of whom the sants sang was devoid enough of mythic attributes to be as conceivably Islamic as he was Hindu, by the time the sants began to flourish toward the middle of the fifteenth century they were attracting large segments of a natively Hindu Indian population. By Palṭū's day in the eighteenth century most sants would come from middle Hindu castes.

Palṭū himself was born a baniyā—the stereotypical Hindu shopkeeper—and turns the tradition of the convention-mocking holy man toward the image of his own moderately respectable caste. He sings of the sant as a mad merchant, a profligate giver of spiritual goods:

> Look, there's a merchant gone mad—
> He's running a knowledge shop. (refrain)
>
> He's selling deathless nectar, but still it seems like poison:
> No customers will buy it.
> They ask for salty snacks, he shows them sugar in the raw;
> He looks like he's confused. (1)
> He gives loans without conditions
> And asks everyone to take them.
> Those who do will leave him happy
> And won't ever be asked to pay him back. (2)
> His scales forgive, his weights are full,
> His words are sweet for all.
> With gems of *nām* just lying in piles about
> He weighs them out, and asks no price. (3)
> Of *surat* key and *śabda* lock
> He tells through yogic means.
> Says Palṭū: Truth's a constant bargain
> Offered always day and night. (4)[4]

Though *nām, surat,* and *śabda* in the last verse of the song are all technical terms of yoga, the song does not really dwell on the esoteric side of Palṭū's experience. Rather, it expresses the frustrations of the yogi who is also a popular guru, offering yogic riches to a public absorbed in the ritual traffic of Rām worship at Ayodhyā.

Far to the west of Ayodhyā, at Hāthras, near Agra, a sant named Tulsī Sāhib recognized himself as the reincarnation of Tulsī Dās, who sang the praises of Rām in the great Hindi version of the epic Rāmāyaṇa. Though Tulsī Sāhib's commonly known Rāmāyaṇa is highly conducive to the ceremonial worship of Lord Rām, Tulsī Sāhib in his present incarnation took the heritage of the Hindi sants as an alternative to Hindu ritual worship. In a book called the *Inner Rāmāyaṇa* he elaborates at length on the idea of sant tradition. Arguing one by one with the proponents of established Indian religions, Tulsī Sāhib demonstrates the superiority of *sant mat*, "the teaching of the sants." Through followers of the Radhasoami movement, who inherit a direct spiritual legacy from Tulsī Sāhib, the idea of *sant mat* has become familiar to circles of devotees in the West today.

It was Tulsī Sāhib, living into the nineteenth century, who finally produced a learned exposition of *sant mat;* yet sants had long before seen themselves as constituting some sort of spiritual brotherhood. Just how far the early sants saw themselves within a distinct tradition and in what ways their perceptions of commonality in fact reflected shared practice are by no means settled questions.[5] Some sants appear as notoriously idiosyncratic individuals, and movements bearing sants' names have developed in highly diverse ways. But the ideal of the sant is lauded in verse, later Hindi sants refer to earlier ones, and Kabīr, the first great figure in the Hindi tradition, mentions earlier Marāṭhī predecessors. By the seventeenth century, great sectarian compilations—which include verses in sant style from figures beyond the immediate lineage—testify to ideas of a larger tradition of sants, if imprecisely understood and realized from diverse perspectives. By the end of the nineteenth century Radhasoami groups were formulating ideas of sant tradition that fit nicely into their own theologies.

Whence this idea of sant tradition among even the very first remembered Hindi sants? If disciples truly do locate their sole source of divine grace in the guru—either within or without—what spiritual value do they also find in the idea of a somewhat vague and amorphous tradition? These questions are indicative of a contradiction that stands at the root of the cumulative tradition known to sants. Among contemporary Radhasoamis, where the guru is unmistakably manifest as a living person, this contradiction is particularly blatant. For though disciples are regularly enjoined to take the guru as their primary object of faith, they consistently understand him within a more widely encompassing religious context. And as disciples in any version of sant tradition place the living guru within some larger context, their perception of him changes, itself becoming larger, more profound. To convey power concretely, many say, the guru should ideally be embodied as a living individual. But for his spiritual power to be trustworthy, the guru must seem to be more than an individual human person. Indeed, he must appear in certain ways as a source of supreme grace comparable to others known throughout the religions of the world.

1. Three Immanent Foci of the Divine: The Eternal Heritage, The Singular Personality, and the Holy Man

The world religions teach of different types of sources through which divine grace, knowledge, and power are mediated to humankind. From our perspective, three of these stand out as essential: the eternal heritage, the singular personality, and the holy man. Mediation through the eternal heritage is perceived as the assimilation of the ageless wisdom underlying the accumulated tradition of a people. Mediation through the singular personality comes through participation in a universal fount of grace established on earth by a divine being, which is often accessible though a teaching and a sacrament he has left. Mediation through the holy man is experienced as a direct communication from a living person qualified to transmit the divine. Conceived according to different understandings of the way in which spiritual power finds a center on earth, each of these sources represents a particular perception of the *immanent focus* of the divine.

The scene at Palṭū's Ayodhyā presents us with all three immanent foci. Pilgrims bathe in the sacred waters, where brahmins, reciting mantras, invoke the power of the eternal Hindu heritage. Intimately in houses and shops, magnificently in major temples, Rām the singular personality displays his image throughout the town, attracting pilgrims from all over the subcontinent. Rejecting both the value of priestly ritual and the glory of Rām's image, Palṭū the mad merchant, himself a holy man, dispenses spiritual gifts to his disciples.

The three ways of access to the divine seen here in Hindu Ayodhyā find parallels in other religious traditions throughout the world. As brahmins practice the elaborate ritual observances prescribed in their sacred books, so observant Jews practice the law discussed endlessly in theirs. Experienced through the specific forms of venerable cultures, the eternal heritages of both Hinduism and Judaism reveal the divine as something ancient, the birthright of those born to the tradition. The religions finding their sources in the teachings of Jesus, Buddha, and Muhammad, by contrast, are able to transcend cultural environments. Their founding figures stand as unique sources of grace, and even more than Rām at

Ayodhyā, attract people from all over. When experienced through any of these figures, the divine demands a conscious acceptance of a specific personality and teaching, and is revealed as something more magnificent and boundless than ancient and "ours." The holy man, for his part, reveals the divine as something spontaneous, paradoxical, and palpably powerful. Like the erratic Palṭū, Hasids, Sufis, and Zen masters are notorious for demanding both patience and trust from their disciples.

The characteristic responses elicited by the immanent foci vary according to the contexts in which the foci appear. And the immanent foci usually do present themselves in combination. The disciple of the Zen master reveres both the personality of the Buddha as the source of enlightenment and the enigmatic holy man who enlightens him personally. The noble and virtuous personality worshipped by the devotee of Rām in fact embodies cherished family ideals of the Hindu heritage. And as the Hindu (but not the Judaic) heritage offers a panoply of personalities to adore, so may a world religion focused on a singular personality evolve catholic traditions in which the cumulative ritual and textual heritage itself is seen to mediate the divine. We can, then, begin to compare diverse traditions as configurations of foci in different contexts. But to understand the dynamic through which these configurations take shape, we must identify more precisely the distinctive characteristics of the immanent foci themselves.

a. The Distinctive Characteristics of the Immanent Foci

As a type of *place* through which the divine is seen to be mediated, each immanent focus demonstrates distinctive *spatial* characteristics. As a source of divine manifestation does it appear concentrated or diffuse? Is it accessible only to a limited group of people, or is its range potentially limitless? To understand the power of these distinctions, we can return to the scene at Ayodhyā.

The eternal heritage of Hinduism makes its presence felt not only in the public places of Ayodhyā—the pilgrims by the river, the sādhūs on the streets, the temples everywhere—but also in people's homes. Family relationships, personal hygiene, and the preparation of food are all ideally carried out in accordance with complex ritual and legal traditions. In an orthodox Jewish home the stress may fall more on law than on ritual, but the scope of tradition within everyday life is just as extensive. An eternal heritage, then, is pervasive within all the aspects of a culture; the focus it presents is diffuse. Yet precisely because a heritage comes through the forms of a particular culture, it is accessible only to the members of that culture. And this, we are told, is as it should be, for the heritage belongs primarily to those with rights to it by birth. Thus the range of the eternal heritage, both in practice and theory, is limited.

Within its limits, however, the eternal heritage is able to subsume the other foci with ease. For in its diffuseness the heritage appears as many concrete points of focus, all linked together through an eternal mythic nexus. The bathing ghats on the river Saryū, the temples by the ghats, and the priests in the temples all derive meaning from the significance of King Rām's story in the entire complex of Indian lore. To the extent that he is experienced within the whole of the cultural tradition, Rām the singular personality stands in the eternal heritage of Hinduism. And to the extent that the living brahmin priest uses ritual means to link the individual to this mythic reality, he is more of a focal point in the heritage than an independent holy man.

Palṭū, on the other hand, mocking the images and rituals of Ayodhyā, sets himself apart from the Hindu heritage. As a potentially innovative living person, the holy man can himself be experienced as a focus of the divine. But the focus he presents differs crucially from that presented by the external heritage. Self-contained and offering meanings on his own authority, the holy man presents a highly concentrated manifestation. His range of influence, correspondingly, is restricted to those who have been recognized by him personally, and is thus more narrowly limited than the finite cultural domain of the eternal heritage.

In contrast to both the heritage and the holy man, the singular personality offers a potentially unlimited focus. The story of Lord Rām of Ayodhyā is known throughout the Indian subcontinent and Southeast Asia, and stories and teachings of Jesus, Buddha, and Muhammad have spread throughout the world. Presenting himself through a definite mythic personality and a fixed scripture, the singular personality, like the holy man, offers a concentrated focus—though less changeable than the holy man's and subject to more elaborate interpretation.

Historically considered, there are visible continuities between the singular personality and the holy man. A hero named Rām, some say, may once have lived in the world as a king, and few question the historical existence of Jesus, Buddha, and Muhammad.

All the latter figures are remembered to have walked the earth as holy men during their lifetimes—some more innovative and iconoclastic than others. Yet after their passing, all have been revered by devotees as highly exalted divine beings.

From our perspective, whether these beings are perceived as gods or exceptional men—even the very fact of their historical existence—is of less importance than the unique cosmic status claimed for them now. What crucially defines the singular personality is that he be conceived as one of a kind—not as a prophet like any other, nor a member of a class of nameless angels or gurus. Thus, within a moderately diffuse heritage, a singular personality appears as one of a relatively small number of beings whose distinctive divine personal qualities a particular individual may revere—or adore: for a Hindu, most of the great pan-Indian deities together with a few who are important in his region; for a Catholic, Jesus and Mary along with the particular saints to whom he may habitually turn. A singular personality of this sort is usually seen as a uniquely important being to whom access should be universally available.

Sometimes, moreover, living persons are granted this unique cosmic status—special personages like popes, avatars, or sectarian leaders. Often, their roles are presented as distinct relationships to unique historical or mythic beings: the pope to Peter and Jesus, the avatar to Viṣṇu. In any event, the cosmic status of these special personages, while perhaps temporary, is extraordinary as long as it lasts. It is, further, usually unique—like that of the singular personality himself.

The same collectively recognized spiritual image can appear as a different type of immanent focus to different religious individuals. A figure taken respectfully by one individual as a guru, a holy man, may be glorified by another as an avatar—who is at least a very special personage, more likely a singular personality. A deity to whom one individual can relate as a magnificent, complex personality is seen by another as merely belonging to a class of rather manipulable godlings in a heritage. The immanent foci, then, do not refer directly to external objects. Certainly, people in the same tradition have similar experiences of their common objects of faith, which may then attain constant local values. The immanent foci, however, are here offered explicitly as categories of religious perception.

And as categories of religious perception, the immanent foci reveal the divine in distinctive conceptual dimensions. The embodied holy man is powerfully concentrated in man's world, but has a scope limited to men who recognize him. The magnificent singular personality, more permanently concentrated in the heavens, has a scope spreading infinitely to all. In contrast to both, the eternal heritage is spread diffusely through the sacred aspects of a culture, but like the holy man has a limited scope—in this case one restricted to those who have assimilated that culture. At an abstract level, then, the immanent foci can be contrasted to each other through two sets of distinctive characteristics: their manifestation in the world, which can be concentrated or diffuse, and the scope of their potential reach, which can be limited or unlimited.

Distinguishing the three immanent foci in terms of two pairs of binary opposites logically suggests the possibility of a fourth focus, diffuse and unlimited, a unifying truth underlying the forms of all religions. This perception of the divine seems to become particularly important during periods of cultural contact and possible confusion. Certainly, it underlies many of the theosophies of the present day, and came to the fore as well during the age of Hindu-Muslim impact that gave rise to the sants. Nevertheless, while a unifying truth may be familiar to mystics and philosophers, it does not by itself support any large-scale religious tradition. It will thus not need as full a presentation as will be given to the other foci. Yet with its diffuse and limitless characteristics it can appear in many different contexts, and is frequently met, together with other foci, in complex configurations.

When foci appear in configurations we can usually discern some form of balance among them, the limitless scope of one complementing the limited scope of another, a diffuse manifestation balancing a concentrated one. And in looking more closely at the ways in which the foci presented by a tradition become foundations for community and personal religious life, we will see a more complex dynamic among them: that between their hidden and revealed dimensions.

b. The Complementarity between the Hidden and the Revealed

Each of the immanent foci presents the believer with characteristic bases of personal salvation and religious community. Some of these the believer can point to as revealed, with concrete embodiments on earth. Others he knows as hidden, visible only to the eye of the faithful. The revealed and hidden aspects of the immanent foci are outlined in figure 1.

The singular personality, for example, normally offers a basis of salvation in a specific communication from the divine, a definite teaching. The essence of this teaching is frequently revealed in a single holy book that presents the personality's holy life and words:

Eternal Heritage

basis of personal salvation: ancient knowledge		basis of religious community: ancient ways	
revealed: received myth and ritual	hidden: esoteric wisdom	revealed: developed customary law	hidden: organic order of the divine

Singular Personality

basis of personal salvation: saving communication from the divine		basis of religious community: sacred institution	
revealed: holy book	hidden: saving power	revealed: sacramental tradition	hidden: the elect, the true church

Holy Man

basis of personal salvation: spiritual aid		basis of religious community: holy man's personal authority	
revealed: the master's discourse and example	hidden: esoteric help	revealed: the master's orders	hidden: the master's mission

Unifying Truth

basis of personal salvation: the one divine truth		basis of religious community: the brotherhood of all men	
revealed: all scriptures	hidden: their correct interpretation	revealed: all traditions	hidden: the secret brotherhood of the wise

Figure 1.—The Hidden and Revealed Dimensions of the Immanent Foci.

the Rāmāyaṇa, the Gospels. But through their saving power, Rām, Jesus, and the Buddha may also remain accessible in a hidden form, continuing to communicate divine truths and to hear the prayers of devotees.

The basis of religious community offered by a singular personality is generally some sort of sanctified institution, from Rāmānandī sectarians to the Catholic Church. Revealed, this institution presents itself in a sacramental institution and the power of its administrators; hidden, as Calvin knew, it appears as the elect of the Lord, the true divine church.

The relatively compact bases of personal salvation and religious community, teachings and churches potentially available to all, present a contrast to those found within an eternal heritage. Diffuse and complex, the eternal heritage offers differing avenues of approach to people of different social status and personal temperament. The basis of personal salvation offered by an eternal heritage lies in the ancient knowledge of a people. Revealed in the forms of myth and ritual familiar to all, this ancient knowledge may nevertheless present facets more appropriate for certain people and situations than for others. Thus, all with roots in the heritage can make a pilgrimage to the Saryū at Ayodhyā or the temple at Jerusalem, but only the born priest is fit to administer the ritual. Yet since the ancient knowledge presents its hidden aspect in forms of secret, esoteric wisdom reserved only for a few, many pay more profound reverence to the yogi or Kabbalist than to the brahmin or Kohen. Indeed, behind the customary law that serves as the revealed basis for community life, the wise see a hidden order, divine and organic. It was this order that the sages understood in pronouncing the laws of the glorious past—when Rām ruled virtuously at Ayodhyā and the temple stood in Jerusalem.

These diffuse bases of salvation and community offered by a heritage frequently find an important practical complement in the image of a singular personality. Indeed, within a highly diverse heritage like Hinduism a singular personality can play a vital particularizing function. Thus, for many, Rām is less a virtuous king of old than a compelling divine personality, an object of personal devotion providing a concentrated focus for meticulous ritual practice. Elements of common ritual revealed to all, when thus focused in a singular personality, serve to deliver his particular saving power.

Out of the elements of a complex heritage, a well defined sectarian community may take shape, cherishing scriptures revealed in the name of a specific personality. These, understood to disclose the secrets of the heritage's hidden order, will highlight a particular orientation among the many ethical options that a diverse tradition has to offer. The virtues of family and civic duty idealized in the epic of Rām thus stand in dramatic contrast to the rapturous abandonment of the world for the divine evoked in verses of Krishna devotion.

Conversely, the compact bases of salvation and community offered by the singular personality begin to reach different kinds of people at their own levels as a diverse heritage develops. The sacraments of the Roman Church make the workings of grace appear manifest at important junctures in the life cycle; and its ritual can let the power of Jesus and the saints play in the everyday lives of men all over the world. In its religious orders, moreover, the Church encompasses communities that offer options suited to different types of especially motivated individuals. Living according to codified rules revealed by saints of the past, people within monastic communities are able to ponder esoteric mysteries hidden deep within their heritage.

Occasionally in the Catholic hierarchy an individual arises like Nicholas de Cusa, the fifteenth-century cardinal and man of letters who speculated about the possibility of esoteric truth in traditions other than his own.[6] Yet this vision of a unifying truth has usually been more prevalent in India, and in different ways has informed the perspective of many sants. However generous they are as spiritual insights, ideas about the one divine truth underlying all religions and the universal brotherhood of all men can only with difficulty form the basis for a coherent religious tradition. Certainly, an attempt to embrace the revealed scriptures and sacraments of many diverse traditions at once will lead to confusion and inconsistency. Religious communities with a highly unifying focus must then find a necessary coherence in the hidden side of the unifying truth. Scriptures must be given their correct, secret interpretation; a select brotherhood of the wise must be singled out, who know what the inherent unity of all men really means.

A vision of a unifying truth thus provides a fertile context for the holy man, since it is he who knows the hidden meaning of diverse scriptures and can initiate disciples into the select brotherhood of the wise. In the holy man, then, a unifying truth finds a necessary defining complement.

In whatever context the holy man is found, the basis of personal salvation he offers is usually seen as some sort of definite spiritual help, revealed in his discourse and example. But the living guru's outward behavior can be baffling and unpredictable. For Palṭū, more consistently reliable than the outward guru as "mad merchant," may have been the guru's image within, which "overspread his heart." Thus, frequently taken to be more important than the holy man's revealed discourse and example is his hidden esoteric help, the inner riches that the guru gives, however eccentric he may appear on the surface.

Such religious community as the holy man offers is based in his personal authority, and its everyday activity is regulated by his explicitly revealed orders, often demanding and impenetrable. Nevertheless, a vision of their guru's hidden mission may help his disciples persevere in their allegiance, and give the group a coherent, independent direction.

The mission of the holy man and the meaning of the help he offers is given definition through the greater context in which he stands. Within an eternal heritage the holy man finds a place as a conduit of ancient hidden wisdom, revealing the true relationship between customary tradition and the natural order of the divine. In a wider religious context focused on a singular personality the holy man may be understood to carry on that personality's mission in the world at present. His esoteric help is then taken as a concrete manifestation of the personality's saving power. Holy men proclaiming highly inclusive unifying truths, finally, are understood to know the mysteries of all the world's religions.

But what happens to any dynamic equilibrium among the foci in sant tradition, where figures like Palṭū and Kabīr have little use for either the Hindu heritage or the legacy of Muhammad? In what does the highly concentrated manifestation and limited scope of the holy man find a complement? Many later devotees clearly did seem to look beyond the holy man alone, forging their own versions of sant tradition out of familiar Indic ritual heritages and the personalities of great sants of the past. The next chapter will contrast some of the different problems that emerged in traditions stemming from gurus in Palṭū's extended lineage. But before we contrast those traditions as configurations of foci, we will first consider the practical implications of the values that the immanent foci present.

c. Spiritual Values and Practical Problems

Crucial to the way an individual expresses his perception of an immanent focus is the type of spiritual value he sees it manifesting in space and time. In its spatial aspect, the eternal heritage is taken to be pervasive in everyday life; the singular personality, with an unlimited scope and with no equal in the cosmos, appears to be for everyone everywhere; the holy man seems close at hand, effective, "with us here." In its temporal aspect, the heritage appears both ancient and eternal; the singular personality historically unique; and the holy man aware of current spiritual realities, present, "with us now."

If acted upon in practical circumstances, however, each of these values leads to its own type of problems. In space, such problems entail making distinctions. The pervasiveness of an eternal heritage throughout a cultural sphere leads to the necessity of distinguishing the ways in which different classes and individuals may properly participate in the heritage. The stratified castes of Hindu India thus find their counterparts in the codified family relationships of Confucian China. The singular personality, a unique focus over diverse cultures, needs to maintain some distinctness within often highly varied traditional idioms. What common source remains visible behind the diverse world development of Buddhism, Christianity, or Islam? Each particular holy man needs to be understood as a distinct spiritual individual with his own special qualities, capacities, and limits. One sant, when well known, is not like any other.

Temporal problems, on the other hand, involve adaptation. The forms of an eternal heritage must adapt to the oncoming present and future (problems of "tradition and change"); the appearance of a singular personality as a unique cosmic event requires an adaptation of past history (understanding the Church as the "new Israel"); the holy man with a mortal body and finite mind, constantly adapting to changing circumstance, presents problems of immediate continuity in religious perception.

An examination of what the foci as bases of individual salvation and religious community imply in space and time then yields four broad categories of religious phenomena. For individual religious life, the perception of an immanent focus in space leads to a vision of the divine, emotive factors, and types of practice; in time it leads to speculation about how the divine has come to take an immanent form and what one can do to be saved—general problems of theology. A community's collective understanding of a particular focus in space informs its modes of internal coherence and its place in society; in its temporal aspect, this perception informs the com-

	Individual Life		Values and Problems	Religious Community	
Space	specific forms of myth and ritual for different types of situations	cosmic meaning can be seen in all facets of everyday life	values: "pervades our culture" problems: distinguishing religious roles within a culture	whole societies participate, but different sections in different ways	conflicts in customary law can be resolved through intuitions of cosmic order
Revealed and Hidden Bases	revealed: received myth and ritual	hidden: esoteric wisdom	**eternal heritage**	revealed: developed customary law	hidden: natural order of the divine
Time	established rituals explained in terms of mythological past	changing circumstances seen in terms of past causes	values: ancient, eternal problems: adapting to impending circumstances	gradual process of adaptation leads to eventual disintegration of culture or successful assimiilation of new forms	enforcing the pristine cosmic order leads to purifying isolation or aggressive pursuit of manifest destiny

Figure 2.—Phenomena Characteristically Derived from a Perception of the Eternal Heritage.

munity's dynamic of continuity and change. Figures 2, 3, and 4 present the religious phenomena elicited by the immanent foci as the results of interaction between the bases of salvation and community the foci offer and the spatial and temporal problems they pose.

The reader examining these three charts will probably be able

	Individual Life		Values and Problems	Religious Community	
Space	liturgical worship deriving from scripture	personal prayer to magnificent Lord	values: “for everyone” problems: maintaining his own distinctness	world-scale institutions provide common standards	elect groups maintain their own rigorous standards
Revealed and Hidden Bases	revealed: holy book	hidden: saving power	**singular personality**	revealed: sacramental tradition	hidden: the elect, the true church
Time	doctrines of final revelation	doctrines of the personality's everlasting grace	values: for all time problems: adapting past traditions	sectarian leaders make practical decisions about tradition and change	members of the true church can retreat from the world or become subversive within it

Figure 3.—Phenomena Characteristically Derived from a Perception of the Singular Personality.

to think easily enough of concrete examples for the eternal heritage and the singular personality. Examples for the holy man, however, may not be so readily forthcoming. Nevertheless, traditions in most large-scale religious contexts have at times produced figures powerful enough to yield some of the forms characteristic of the holy man in space: charismatic leaders to whom allegiance, obedience, or devotion is offered by a limited group of disciples, often instructed in specific religious practice. Like Palṭū, many of these figures are famous for the paradoxical images they project and the esoteric instructions they offer.

The world religions may also encompass sustained traditions of the holy man in time. Yogic traditions within Hinduism and Buddhism have long flourished in India, while lineages of Hasids, Sufis, and Zen masters present parallel traditions in their respective world religions. Members of these traditions have further speculated on the role of the holy man within the divine scheme of salvation in terms that their greater religious contexts provide. And in so doing they have articulated the elements of a theology of the holy man within their different world religions.

By contrast, the early Hindi sants as holy men often attempted

	Individual Life		Values and Problems	Religious Community	
Space	spontaneous holy man reveals divine as immediate, changeable, paradoxical	the master instructs through situations, intervenes psychically, and initiates into specific technique	values: "with us here" problems: to be understood as a distinct individual	all disciples respond immediately to master's overt commands	select disciples can intuit what the master really wants to be done
Revealed and Hidden Bases	revealed: outward example and discourse	hidden: esoteric help	**holy man**	revealed: expressed commands of the master	hidden: the master's cosmic mission
Time	the master's discourses and example present constantly new revelation	[doctrines of the continuing saving power of holy men on earth?]	values: "with us now" problems: continuity in tradition	limited scope of master's expressed commands gives community marginal role in society; but their immediate wisdom gives it a potentially seminal one	perfected disciples carry on the master's work

Figure 4.—Phenomena Characteristically Derived from a Perception of the Holy Man.

to place themselves outside the context of any world religion. Few seemed to care about maintaining the forms of established tradition or enunciating explicit theological formulae. But explicit examples of a sant theology can be found in later stages of the tradition. Some of the most lucid examples came from the Radhasoami gurus, who were often educated gentlemen. Yet as theologies of holy men, the doctrines of these gurus eventually prove ambiguous. Indeed, nowhere in the history of religions have we been able to find a large-scale, developed theology deriving from the perception of the holy man alone, unrelated to other foci. Thus in figure 4, brackets have been placed around the entry that would include doctrines of the holy man's continuous saving power—doctrines potentially deriving from the perception of the holy man in time.

The recurrent anomaly we see in sant tradition, then, here appears as a disparity between the potentials of the holy man as focus in space and as focus in time. Certainly, disciples finally are able to come to terms with an enigmatic figure like Palṭū as a trustworthy and visible source of grace. As a focus in space, he thus appears comparable to both the images of Rām and the brahminic ritual surrounding him in Ayodhyā. Yet he is not, like Rām, an avatar of Viṣṇu, who incarnates periodically to save the world from disaster; nor does he, like a ritualistic brahmin, carry the weight of a heritage stemming from an ancient divine source. How can the salvational role of the holy man in history be understood? How can community be sustained through the generations by the type of leadership he provides?

2. Religious Traditions as Configurations of Foci in Contexts

Answers to these questions entail an understanding of the ways in which the sants participated in the worlds of meaning that both they and their disciples knew. The historical, social, cultural, and broader religious environments of the sant not only contribute to his significance in the eyes of the devotee but also shape the religious phenomena that the sant elicits as focus. Our comparative framework can distinguish at least three major classes of contexts, each giving specific significance to a focus in its own way: religio-cultural contexts, socio-historical ones, and those deriving from the greater religious traditions in which the foci stand.

Religio-cultural contexts include broad styles of piety and

underlying idioms within a particular cultural area. Pervading much of North Indian religion, for example, is a cultural idiom of flowing substance that permeates individuals, as well as two different styles of piety—devotional and yogic. These two styles of piety may lead to traditions very different from each other: the pietistic ritual devotion of Ayodhyā is quite distinct from the rough tantric practice known in yogic traditions also contemporaneous with Palṭū. Religio-cultural contexts, however, at the same time frequently overlap, so Palṭū can both rapturously contemplate his guru and brusquely tell of "yogic means."

To express his yogic triumphs, moreover, Palṭū occasionally borrows metaphors from his socio-historic environment.

The one who can set free the citadel-body
Is really a Rājpūt
Really a Rājpūt:
He sets fire to the stronghold
And frees entrenched enemy lines
In a flash. . . .[7]

The Rājpūt referred to here is the Hindu warrior-ruler of the India that Palṭū knew. Certainly, the Rājpūt exercised his power within a socio-political order that varied with specific locality and changed over time. Nevertheless, the general post-classical Indian political order itself has been roughly characterized as "feudal" and can be meaningfully compared to similar socio-historical patterns in other parts of the world.

In this way, socio-historical contexts, which encompass matters of social structure and historical circumstance, contrast with religio-cultural ones. Religio-cultural contexts are normally specific to particular contiguous religio-cultural areas, though they frequently demonstrate long continuities over time. Socio-historic contexts, on the other hand, change more rapidly, but lend themselves more readily to comparisons across disparate cultures. Factors of "culture" and "society," then, both provide contexts that inform specific religious traditions. Certainly, attention to each type of context is necessary for a full understanding of the verses of Palṭū that we have seen. But Palṭū consciously rejects the scriptural, sacramental, and mythological resources of the greater religious contexts familiar to him. Thus problematic in sant tradition, this third type of context is particularly deserving of our study.

North India presents us with greater religious contexts deriving from Hinduism, Buddhism, and Islam. In Hinduism, for example, we find Vaiṣṇavas and Śaivas developing their own contexts of myth and scripture; in Islam we find Sunnis and Shi'is looking to different heroes and adopting different legal codes. These broad contexts encompass more specific but still large traditions: Hindu Vaiṣṇavas of the Rāmānandī sect; Muslim Sunni Naqshbandīs.

We can treat the world religions themselves—"Islam," "Hinduism," "Christianity"—as the "greatest" of greater religious contexts. For taken as world religions they certainly appear less as relatively coherent, functioning religious institutions than as great contexts providing sets of meanings that inform many, often very different, specific traditions. In a given cultural area, world religious contexts can overlap conspicuously with religio-cultural contexts—and it may in fact be the latter that are most crucial for characterizing the practice of specific traditions. Thus a Hindu *tantrika* and a Buddhist *tantrika* have at least as much in common with each other as either does with an ordinary observant householder of his own persuasion.

Greater religious contexts (and the world religions as the greatest of these) do, however, offer much more than a scriptural, sacramental, and mythological idiom. They also offer the individual the elements of a sectarian identity. Thus, within the broad Śaiva and Śākta traditions of Hindu tantra we find local schools with their own allegiances; among Buddhist *tantrikas* in Tibet, lineages looking back to Milarepa, Padmasambhāva and others—each with its own featured hagiographies and scriptures. Perhaps even more important for our investigation, these contexts give the holy man within them a greater cosmic identity: native Tibetan ritual, as well as tha tantric lama, represent the "teachings of the Buddha"; the Hindu guru might be seen as essentially one with Śiva—and both Śiva and the guru as knowing the "eternal Vedic truths."

A specific tradition, then, may be situated in a greater context through an identification of its distinctive focus with that of the greater context. So if, in general, we say that religio-cultural contexts relate directly to factors of personal religious life, and sociohistorical contexts to factors of religious community, then the greater religious contexts relate directly to the foci themselves. They present successive layers of cumulative tradition, each often having its own focus. Traditions then may present configurations of foci, each focus drawn from a greater, more broadly encompassing context.

Every focus in a configuration is likely play a different role. The dominant focus of a specific tradition is usually close to its inner core. But the configuration as a whole is frequently given shape, at least in part, by one of the outer, "greater," contextual strata. Look, for example, at the Hindu *tantrikas* of Kaśmīr. Around the guru, his disciples, and his lineage we can identify at least three significant strata of greater religious contexts: the greatest is Hinduism generally, then Śaivism, and finally Kaśmīrī Śaivism as a school.

Hinduism generally provides a focus in the "Vedic" heritage, with its developed ritual forms and Vedantic philosophies. As an informing context, Hinduism usually ensures that the traditions within it maintain their full ritual patrimony, but beyond that it lets them develop as they will (in contrast, say, to Judaism, a considerably more restrictive informing heritage). The singular personality of Śiva provides the yogi with both a complex focus for devotion and a source of mystical experience. Kaśmīrī Śaivism appears as a specific heritage within Śaivism, with its own scriptures, practices, and heroes.

Since every component of this configuration of foci around the guru has its own role, each can in fact turn out to be crucial for different individuals in different circumstances. The guru, as the dominant focus, provides the basis for such community as exists in yogic traditions. He is also likely to appear as the principal basis of personal salvation for most of his disciples most of the time. If asked why they look to their guru for salvation these disciples might say something like: "The ancient texts cannot be truly understood, nor Śiva known, without the guru's grace." An individual particularly impressed by the magnificent image of Śiva as singular personality, however, may consistently look to him: "I feel Śiva controlling my spiritual life." Someone only casually involved in the circle, or temporarily disaffected from the guru, may have somewhat different reasons for taking the singular personality as primary object of faith: "Well, all gurus are Śiva anyway." Still others, especially adept at a specific traditional practice, may think that it is the richness of their heritage that finally counts: "Our Kaśmīrī sages really knew what they were talking about"; or "This mantra from the Vedas really works."

The disciples of the tantric yogi, then, able to draw on such a wide range of explicit contexts to give superhuman status to their guru, have an easier time dealing with the holy man's finiteness than do the disciples of a sant. Nevertheless, the disciples of the sant are not without their resources. For the idea of sant tradition has itself generated the basis for a greater religious context, one able to encompass individual gurus within the ever greater circles of meaning that the mystery of the sant can suggest.

NOTES

/1/ The "eighth of the heavens" and the "stream of oil" are frequent expressions of Palṭū. The poet speaks of "sounds in the sky" in *Palṭū Sāhib kī Bānī*, 3 vols. (Allahabad: Belvedere Press, 1965–67) 2:71 and 3:1.
/2/ *Palṭū Bānī:* 3:1.
/3/ *Palṭū Bānī:* 3:2–3.
/4/ *Palṭū Bānī:* 3:73.
/5/ For more on different scholarly interpretations of sant tradition see my *Lord as Guru*, p. 5.
/6/ See *De Pace Fidei,* translated by John P. Dolan in *Unity and Reform* (South Bend, Indiana: University of Notre Dame Press), 1962, pp. 195–237.
/7/ *Palṭū Bānī* 1:43.

CHAPTER 2

WHO IS THE GURU AT GOVIND SĀHIB'S SHRINE?

Not only has the mystery of the guru been comprehended in different ways across the diverse tradition of sants, it may also be realized in different ways within the same local lineage. The distinct patterns of worship, ritual, and lifeways that evolve at separate centers of even a small regional tradition can reflect alternative ideas about the meaning of gurus past and present. As speculation about the place of sants in the continuing economy of salvation, these ideas derive from perceptions of the holy man in time. Thus, in studying the socio-religious manifestations of those perceptions, it makes sense to offer a historical dimension: in what ways do people's attitudes toward holy men and other immanent foci reflect the changing practical realities of their lineage? To highlight contrasts among opposing orientations, the dynamics through which the foci are realized in tradition will be illustrated through an extended sectarian *conflict*.

The dispute at the shrine of Palṭū's guru Govind Sāhib was a provincial affair. It nevertheless presented some of the most dramatic events I encountered during my fieldwork during 1980 and '81. The small stakes of the struggle can make the actors in the narration appear petty in their concerns. Yet the very provinciality of the scene is also revealing: it at once presents the very human perceptions in which the immanent foci are grounded and demonstrates how even small-scale local rivalries can have larger religious dimensions. Thus, while many of the issues of succession that emerged in the dispute are endemic to Hindu sectarian traditions, the dispute itself is not presented as a great classical model that has had lasting reverberations throughout India. It serves instead as a backdrop highlighting some practical implications of the immanent foci: their use as the basis for a morphology of religious life and the ways in which they can help us understand recurrent problems in the history of religions.

While the descriptions offered below derive largely from field experience, the historical narrative is based on written sources. These include two specialized academic works in Hindi[1] and one short history of the shrine and its gurus written by a scholar from inside the tradition.[2] Though the author of the sectarian history, Prabhū Dās, was the chief priest of the Palṭū Akhāṛā at the time of the dispute and himself a protagonist in the events described, he wrote the book well before the dispute took place. The book therefore reflects Prabhū Dās' perspective as a sādhū and scholar in the lineage of Palṭū—not the violent animosities that were in the air in 1980 and '81, when I visited the shrine.

1. The Shrine in its Contexts

Its tower visible from a main road between Faizābād and Āzamgaṛh in Eastern Uttar Pradesh, the shrine to Govind Sāhib is a substantial establishment, well built up over the years. Dominating the shrine complex is a large artificial pool, a welcome sight in the dry plains; surrounding the pool are numerous rooms for visitors and resident sādhūs. In keeping with sant iconoclasm and reverence among sants for a plurality of holy men in tradition, the tomb of Govind Sāhib itself is small and unpretentious, sharing its sanctity with the tomb right next to it of one of Govind Sāhib's immediate successors, Benī. As a lineage center, then, the shrine stands out less through the magnificence of the tombs than through substantial institutional development. The shrine complex houses a local primary school, and recent gurus have sponsored colleges in nearby towns. Regular income for these projects is derived from land attached to the shrine and shops within the complex, which are rented to local merchants and patronized by villagers. Seasonal income, moreover, is generated by a large fair held for two weeks every winter. Tradesmen set up temporary booths, and people come from all over the surrounding districts for the spectacle and shopping as well as for worship. Over the years, the shrine complex has come to overshadow the small village in which it is located, so that the village itself is both known to local people and listed on regional bus routes simply as Govind Sāhib.

In the course of research on sants in the extended lineage in which Palṭū stood, I had gone to investigate the regionally renowned establishment at Govind Sāhib. Getting off the bus from Faizābād and finding my way in from the highway, I encountered a sādhū—a religious mendicant—puttering in a garden, robes pulled up over his knees. Most of the people I had approached in my field investigations had seemed happy to find an excuse to break from work and talk about their religion, but not this fellow. He appeared preoccupied, perhaps caught up in the crisis I would soon discover at the shrine; in any event, he wasn't saying much.

I asked him the way to the temple. He pointed.

I continued: Where could I find the guru? He looked quizzical.

"Which guru?" he asked. Who did I want to talk to? There was no guru there.

I was puzzled. How could such an imposing institution not at least have someone in charge? I questioned the sādhū further: Was there really no guru at all at the shrine? In face of my persistance, the sādhū tried another approach: actually, he said, the shrine had three gurus—but none was around. I soon came to understand that the shrine at Govind Sāhib was caught up in a bitter struggle for succession. The old guru had died suddenly, naming no heir; and when I arrived there were three contenders, all away and gathering their forces.

Revealing sectarian intrigues and the wiles of gurus in a small regional tradition, the succession dispute at Govind Sāhib's shrine also highlights some crucial differences among orientations of religious life and community offered by the principal immanent foci. For whatever personal ambitions motivated the contenders for the guruship, they gained support from interested groups with competing ideas about what the shrine should represent and how its resources should be used. Should the shrine be a place for living holy men to meditate and offer counsel to pious devotees? Should it instead be a place for a community of householders to worship a great personality of the past, served by a renunciate priest of their liking? Or should the educational institutions sponsored by the shrine be nurtured, integrating elements of the Hindu heritage with the modern world? These potential roles for the shrine, moreover, derive their meanings from broad Indian contexts as well as restricted local ones.

Greater religious contexts. The greater Hindu world in which the succession struggle played itself out incorporates pan-Indian, regional, and local traditions. At the same time, the immediate contenders to Govind's shrine identified with a specific lineage of sants. All of these traditions—broadly based and narrowly provincial, orthodox Hindu and heterodox sant—added their own significance to the particular visions of the immanent foci that came to the fore at the time of the dispute.

The most encompassing of the greater religious contexts is the ritual heritage of Hinduism as it had evolved in post-classical times. Though the common element in all traditions known as Hindu is a self-understanding that they are derived from the Vedas, after the collapse of classical Hindu empire in the middle of the first millenium A. D. Vedic rituals ceased to be performed on any large scale. Ritual practice, however, remained; brahmins were needed to perform it; and a hierarchical caste structure with brahmins at the head was the pervasive socio-religious environment that even lineages of sants could not for long escape. Govind Sāhib himself had been born a brahmin, and before he found his guru in sant tradition he had made his living as a ritual officiant and public teller of edifying myth. Local brahmins frequented the shrine—dedicated to one of their own—carried out rituals there, and formed a party in the succession dispute.

Not only caste-conscious and ritualistic, post-classical Hinduism was also devotional. As a place of worship, the shrine to Govind Sāhib competed with a great many temples to divinities of lesser and greater renown. Indeed, to some among the later generations of devotees, Govind Sāhib and a few of his successors themselves appeared as great personalities, approaching the rank of Hindu gods. In the image of which deity would these imposing lineage personalities most often be seen by their followers? Though all the great gods of the Hindu pantheon had their devotees in the region, the most important personality was clearly Rām, whose legendary capital of Ayodhyā lay not far distant. Rām and his pilgrimage center at Ayodhyā would thus provide an important regional context for the history of the shrine. During the heyday of Govind as a singular personality, the shrine would be presented as comparable in sanctity to Ayodhyā. During the time of the dispute, the Palṭū Akhāṛā established at the Hindu pilgrimage center would present a contrasting focus of lineage tradition.

The lineage tradition itself found historical origins in the sants' devotion to living gurus, who emerged as vital objects of worship during the post-classical era. These post-classical holy men were more idiosyncratic and rough than Upanishadic seers of earlier times, who were depicted as having distilled the inner meaning of the Vedic ritual heritage.[3] While the earlier seers had maintained reverence for the ways of the heritage, many of the post-classical holy men did not. In addition to gurus versed in learned tantric traditions that seemed to invert traditional norms, both Buddhism and Hinduism knew miracle-working popular figures who exulted in revealing the hypocrisy of long-revered ways.[4] Even as the shrine at Govind Sāhib appeared to elevate a singular personality and become absorbed in a Hindu heritage, it continued to make a place for the charismatic holy man. The persistence of the holy man at the shrine may be explained in part through his roots in both the socio-historical and religio-cultural contexts of post-classical times.

Socio-historical contexts. Broad continuities in the social and political institutions of India stretch back more than a millennium from early modern times.[5] The beginning of this long post-classical era was signalled by the downfall of Harṣa's kingdom in the middle of the seventh century and the subsequent disappearance of large-scale Indian empire. Political power became widely diffused, in the hands of feudal potentates who fought incessantly and were liable to fall. The new political structures that emerged—sometimes styled "feudal"—no doubt contributed to the popular acceptance of holy men as bases of faith that had flourished during the period: if political power is visible and close at hand, demanding loyalty to individuals, then why not spiritual power, too? Cross-cultural comparisons seem to confirm the power of this socio-religious logic, for throughout the history of religions the emergence of a decentralized political structure seems to go hand in hand with the efflorescence of holy men as bases of faith for large numbers of people. We find Zen Masters in Tokugawa Japan and the rise of charismatic Christian saints in late Western antiquity.[6] But in Hindu India this socio-historical context of diffuse political power was colored by particular religio-cultural meanings.

Religio-cultural contexts. Our understanding of the reality known to Hindus has been greatly deepened over the last decade through anthropological work on India that attempts to describe the world in terms of native categories, an approach sometimes referred to as ethno-sociological.[7] Hindus, we are shown, see their universe as a continuum of substance, from the highest consciousness-substance of the ethereal realms to the densest physical matter on earth. All individual entities are permeable, including human beings; and since subtler substances inhere even in physical matter—which can communicate them—people must look very carefully at those with whom they associate. From the conservative perspective known to brahmins, this vision of the world makes sense of the ritual attitudes implied by caste division: different gradations in subtle matter imply different gradations in physical matter, which are acquired at birth. Keeping pure demands keeping separate, interacting only with those of equivalent caste—particularly in regard to such basic physical transactions as eating and marriage. From a more devotional stance, however, similar perceptions of permeable beings in a continuous universe may lead to a heightened valuation of individual piety that stands in tension with caste values. If the Lord really is all powerful, he can manifest himself in anyone, no matter what that person's caste status; transmute him or her physically; and make that individual into a channel through which grace from on high can flow to others. Devotees may then worship powerful gurus born in any caste, attempt to lose their individuality in *them,* and through them become one with the highest divine essence. It is in this religio-cultural context that we find the early Hindi sants, who frequently arose from low castes to sing about a divine guru above, of whom they themselves could be seen as embodiments.

2. The Foci in Tradition

By the time we meet Govind and Palṭū in the eighteenth century, the great early sants had become respectable in the eyes of middle-caste Hindus, who—as both gurus and devotees—had in their turn begun to make their impact felt on the traditions of sants. Govind, Palṭū, and their immediate predecessors in the lineage came largely from reputable Hindu castes. Gurus at the lineage's beginning a century earlier, however, are frequently represented as unorthodox figures. In fact, the succession of gurus in which Govind and Palṭū stand is usually traced back to a woman, not a conventional beginning. This woman sant, moreover, was remembered as so absorbed in the Lord that she acted in explicable ways, absorbed in divine madness. Referred to as Baurī Sāhibā, "Madam Mad Woman," she has lent her name to the lineage in Hindi literary scholarship.

Little is known about Baurī and her male disciple Bīrū, and

they remain as distant, legendary figures, great sants of seventeenth-century Delhi. The lineage emerges in historical light with Bīrū's disciple Yārī, a Muslim with four remembered disciples: two bearing Islamic names and two bearing Hindu ones: One of Yārī's Hindu disciples, Bulla, was a low-caste laborer from the eastern Gangetic plain who eventually returned to his home region, initiating the lineage there. Bulla's first disciple was his employer, a landlord from a martial caste named Gulāl, and with him the lineage becomes transformed from one of mad women, Muslims, and laborers, to one of Hindu men from the twice-born castes of merchants, warriors, and brahmins. Since Gulāl the landlord had the largest local establishment, devotees in the region most often refer to themselves as members of the Gulāl *panth*, the "path" of Gulāl.

The lineage of Baurī Sāhibā is exceptional in sant tradition for the number of notable poets it has produced, and the sectarian development of the Gulāl *panth* reflects the vitality of the independent, creative holy men that have emerged in it. In contrast to some larger sant *panths*, like those of Kabīr and Dādū, which look to a great past sant who has towered over his predecessors, most of the gurus in the principal line of succession of Baurī Sāhibā have been remarkable in their own right. Not only Palṭū, but also Yārī, Bulla, Gulāl, and Bhīkhā (Gulāl's disciple and Govind's guru) have all produced fine sant poetry, much of which has been published. As the glory of the lineage is diffused among its several important sant poets, so sectarian authority within it is decentralized. Four centers have become particularly important. In addition to Govind Sāhib and the Palṭū Akhāṛā in Ayodhyā, which attract devotees from Faizābād and Āzamgaṛh districts, there are two centers in districts somewhat further east: Gulāl's old estate at Bhuṛkuṛā, in Ġāzīpur district, the largest center, where Bulla, Gulāl, and Bhīkhā sat as gurus; and Chitbaṛāgāon, in Balliā, the seat of a disciple of Gulāl named Harlāl, a Kauśik kṣatriya, whose successors continue to draw the allegiance of Kauśiks in the area. Another twelve or fifteen centers, inhabited by one or two or several sādhūs, can be found in the villages of eastern Uttar Pradesh, principally in areas around and between the major centers. Figure 5 shows the main line of succession in the lineage of Baurī together with those of its gurus who will be mentioned as our story unfolds.

The idea that all the establishments founded by gurus in this extended lineage are centers in a single sectarian tradition is clearest in the minds of the *sādhūs* of the Gulāl *panth*, of whom all together

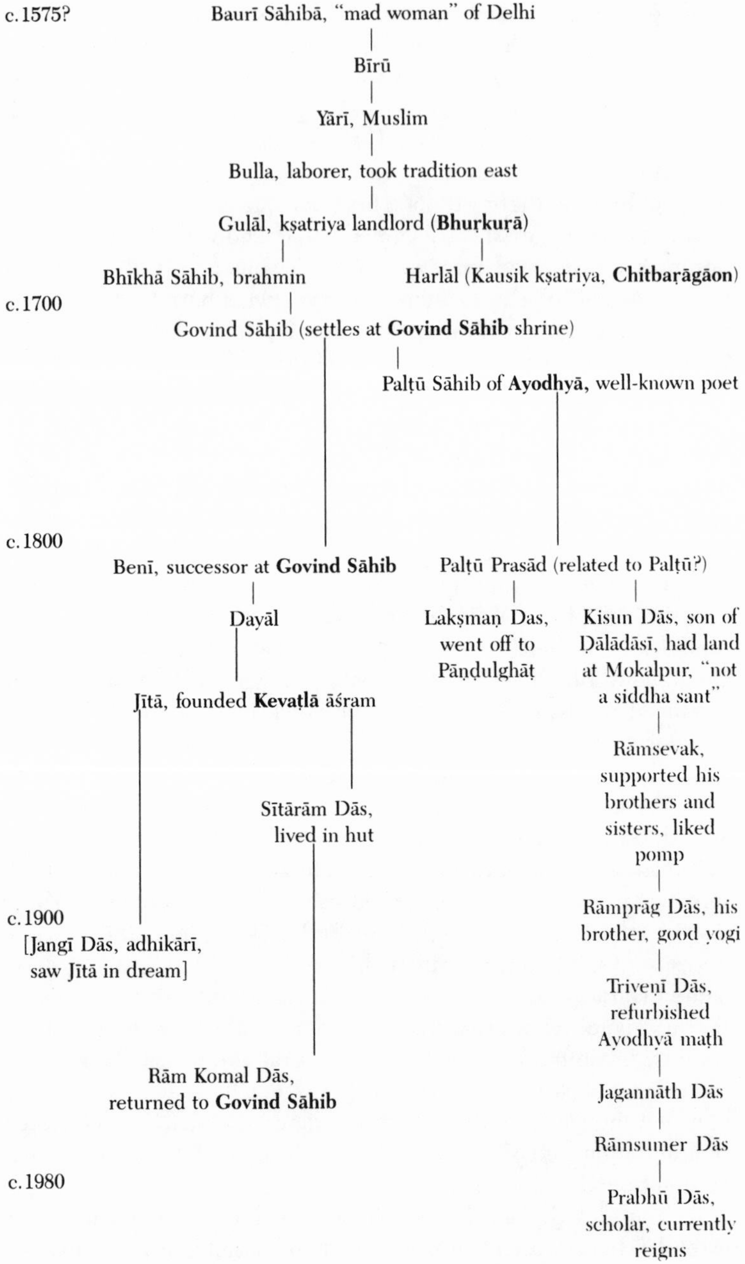
c.1575?
Baurī Sāhibā, "mad woman" of Delhi
Bīrū
Yārī, Muslim
Bulla, laborer, took tradition east
Gulāl, kṣatriya landlord (Bhuṛkuṛā)
Bhīkhā Sāhib, brahmin
Harlāl (Kausik kṣatriya, Chitbaṛāgāon)
c.1700
Govind Sāhib (settles at Govind Sāhib shrine)
Palṭū Sāhib of Ayodhyā, well-known poet
c.1800
Benī, successor at Govind Sāhib
Palṭū Prasād (related to Palṭū?)
Dayāl
Lakṣmaṇ Das, went off to Pāṇḍulghāṭ
Kisun Dās, son of Ḍālādāsī, had land at Mokalpur, "not a siddha sant"
Jītā, founded Kevaṭlā āśram
Rāmsevak, supported his brothers and sisters, liked pomp
Sītārām Dās, lived in hut
c.1900
Rāmprāg Dās, his brother, good yogi
[Jangī Dās, adhikārī, saw Jītā in dream]
Triveṇī Dās, refurbished Ayodhyā maṭh
Rām Komal Dās, returned to Govind Sāhib
Jagannāth Dās
Rāmsumer Dās
c.1980
Prabhū Dās, scholar, currently reigns

Figure 5.—Gurus in the Lineage of Govind

there are probably no more than a hundred or so—the remains of a tradition that seems once to have been more vital.[8] The sādhūs have a few characteristic identifying marks they can employ at ceremonial occasions—a distinctive pattern to use in painting their foreheads as Indian mendicants do, a black wool rosary.[9] Their solidarity is increased through the opportunity they have to travel among the centers—especially at the time of the annual fairs regularly celebrated in commemoration of the founding gurus of shrines both large and small. Householders, on the other hand, less mobile and sometimes moved by communal considerations, are more likely to identify with the sant commemorated at a particular shrine. Thus, as Govind Sāhib is a center for some surrounding brahmins, a local shrine founded by a figure in the lineage of Palṭū—the merchant guru—commands the allegiance of many merchants in a small town I visited in Āzamgaṛh district,[10] who assemble nightly to read Palṭu's verses. Indeed, householders may even refer to themselves not, like the sādhūs, as Gulālpanthīs, but as, say, Govindpanthīs or Palṭūpanthīs, depending on the lineage of the founder of their local shrine.

The different attitudes of sādhūs and householders toward their traditions was a key factor in the succession dispute at Govind Sāhib. The two main parties were on the one hand the sādhūs, whose candidate had been consecrated in the traditional manner by an assemblage of gurus from the other centers, and on the other, householders from Govind's Saryūpārīṇ brahmin caste. Govind Sāhib himself, as well as his successors at the shrine, had been both good sādhūs and born brahmins, and thus had proved acceptable to both parties. At the death of the last mahant—the term for the authoritative successor to a shrine—the leading sādhū was not a brahmin, and the community of renunciates, finding no suitable alternative, chose him. This violated the caste sensibilities of the householders, who were able to locate a brahmin sādhū who had left Govind Sāhib several years before. The latter was, understandably, seen by the sādhūs as a usurper come to take advantage of the situation.

There was bitter enmity between the two sides. With no easy resolution in sight, the principal of one of the colleges sponsored by the shrine appeared as a compromise candidate. Seen as a competent administrator knowledgeable in tradition, someone who could further the institutional interests of the shrine, he had put in his claim to be the mahant before. But since he was not really identified by any influential group as their own, he had gained little substantial support. Thus, while the institutional importance of the shrine made many interested in the dispute, the hard-core support of the two main candidates remained unambiguous: on one side, main-line sādhūs; on the other, influential brahmin householders. There was, however, one exception to this fairly clear dichotomy in tradition: the sādhū mahant of the Palṭū Akkāṛā in Ayodhyā, who sided with the householders. What were the ways in which the temple served the different religious interests of these two groups? And why did the mahant at the Palṭū Akhāṛā differ from the rest of the sādhūs? To answer these questions we will first turn to the history of Govind Sāhib: both the sant of the past and the shrine that bears his name.

a. Govind Sāhib: The Personality and the Shrine

Though most of the great sants have been depicted as unique individuals—holy men with their own inexplicable ways—Govind Sāhib stands out as a highly unusual sant. Both the brahmin caste into which he was born and the imposing shrine that survived his death are exceptional in sant tradition. Together, his caste and his shrine helped transform the figure of Govind into a singular personality of considerable regional import.

Not very many brahmins were attracted to sant tradition during Govind's day in the eighteenth century. The brahmins in sant tradition of whom we hear, moreover, appear much more frequently as gurus and prominent disciples than as ordinary devotees. This preponderance of brahmins as gurus among sants may derive less from their traditional preceptorial role in Indian society than from the probability that sant tradition would draw brahmins who were already religiously exceptional, discontent with ritual ways and prepared to forge ahead on paths of their own. Brahmins who were not as adventurous could turn to religious resources less threatening to their status than sant tradition, which continued to serve devotees largely from low and middle castes. In any event, we are told that Govind Sāhib was disenchanted with his occupation of village priest and preacher and set out on a spiritual quest. Receiving initiation from Bhīkhā, himself a sant of brahmin birth, he returned to his home region, where he was eventually revered as a holy man.

Govind wrote some verses, but he was not highly prolific; he is remembered more as a great spiritual personage of the past than as an important sant poet. Moreover, he is depicted as having been a retiring figure for much of his life as a guru, often consciously avoiding devotees. Since he left no substantial legacy through popular verse or vigorous preaching, Govind's long survival in the memory of people in his home region is surprising. Gurus of greater and lesser distinction have appeared in sant lineages over the centuries; but most have been largely forgotten after a few generations, remembered now only as names in spiritual genealogies. Those known beyond a small circle of devotees are noted either for their poetry or the crucial roles they have played in sectarian history. Govind's works, however, do not compare in popular appeal to those of his disciple Palṭū. He wrote his yogic treatise in Sanskrit—not the commonly accessible Hindi—and his verse in Hindi contains the complex word play found in classical literature, as well as more than the usual number of arcane terms.[11] Nor does Govind present a sectarian figure as striking as that of Palṭū, railing at Ayodhyā orthodoxy. Govind's name, instead, lingers in popular memory largely because of the significance of his shrine.

Indeed, the relationship of Govind Sāhib the person to Govind Sāhib the shrine has neither close parallels in sant tradition nor familiar models in ordinary Hindu practice. Not only is it unusual in India to refer to a village simply by the name of a shrine, it is also unusual in Hindu circles to refer to a shrine simply by the name of a person. One normally speaks instead of a past guru's *samādhi*, a monument that may or may not contain his physical relics. But for most local people, the name Govind Sāhib is primarily that of a place—the site of an impressive artificial pond and exciting annual fair, where children go to school and sādhūs can usually be met. For many local devotees, Govind Sāhib *is* the shrine.

Providing continuity between the figure of Govind the holy man of the historical past, and the shrine as an element in a continuing local religious heritage, is the image of Govind the legendary singular personality. In fact, the stories that come down to us about Govind's life present his biography in three distinct phases. The first is shaped around a discernible historical kernel that reveals some of the social and religious conflicts that might be expected in the life of a brahmin who forsakes his profession to pursue a less orthodox spiritual path. From a wandering holy man in the first years of his spiritual life, Govind turns into an exalted religious personage, a source of pride to the local Hindu community; in this stage he attains the stature of a deity who can perform miracles and grant boons to his devotees. In his last years, finally, Govind retreats into the temple, which then itself bears the weight of a continuing heritage.

i. Govind Sāhib as Holy Man

Govind Sāhib was born in 1727[12] in the village of Jalāpur, near Faizābād in what is now eastern Uttar Pradesh. Like many of the local brahmins, his family was from the Saryūpārīṇ subcaste and known by one of the common brahmin surnames that means "possessing the two Vedas"—"Dvivedī" in its Sanskrit form, or the more common Hindi "Dube."[13] Govind Sāhib's primary education was in Jalāpur, but for further studies he was sent to Banāras, where he stayed for six years. Accomplished in Sanskritic lore and ritual traditions, he returned home to follow his traditional occupation in the village. Govind was particularly skilled as a narrator of mythic lore, and gained a large following for his didactic explanations of the popular Bhāgavat Purāṇa. At the same time, he worked as family priest in the village, performing hallowed Hindu rituals for patrons among the respectable Hindu castes. Among his client families, we are told, was that of Palṭū.

It was Palṭū, they say, who made Govind question the religious value of his brahminic heritage: "It's all very well to hear the tales you tell," Palṭū remarked to Govind, "but it's not the same as experiencing them inwardly."[14] Deeply struck by these words, Govind agreed with Palṭū upon a course of action. The two would travel in different directions searching for truth, and whoever found it first would enlighten the other. Toward the beginning of a pilgrimage to Jagannāth Purī, in the southeast, Govind met Bhīkhā in Bhuṛkuṛā, and eventually took initiation from him.[15] Govind was 34 years old, embarking on a second career as a religious teacher—but now in a very different role than before. From a knowledgeable exponent of the brahminic heritage, a family priest performing ritual, Govind had become a holy man imparting the secrets of yoga and devotion.

Govind is said to have learned many secrets from Bhīkhā: not only the classical yoga of Pantanjali's sutras, which includes practices visible to the external observer—cleansing techniques, postures, and fixing the gaze—but also how to pierce the yogic plexuses within. Yet to keep the divine presence eternally awakened in him, Govind had to experience long periods of lone spiritual practice. There is an old battlemound still visible at Bhuṛkuṛā in which Govind is reported to have sat. Barely big enough to hold one person and admitting only the barest daylight through a small hole, it was to be Govind's abode first for forty days at a stretch, then for longer periods. Subsisting at the beginning on milk and raisins and later, some would say, on nothing at all, Govind achieved his solitary realization. He then returned home to Jalālpur an enlightened, spiritually independent holy man.[16]

Govind in his new enlightened state did not have an easy time in Jalālpur, living at home with his brothers. He was already known from his earlier life as a popular preacher, and his new spiritual influence, we are told, appeared as a threat to the leaders of the Muslim administration of Sorpur, in whose dominion Jalāpur lay. In addition, perhaps, to political pressures, Govind also suffered harassment from his family members, respectable family-priests still revered as *bābās* in some places in the area.[17] Govind tried to help out around the house sometimes, but his behavior was erratic and not always appreciated. The story goes that once Govind was fixing the roof when his sister-in-law appeared in the courtyard and laughed.[18] We are not told whether her laugh was meant to be suggestive or mocking, but it could have been both, and Govind's response was to discourage her by throwing a clod of dirt in her direction. His brother, unfortunately, caught sight of this undignified act, got angry, and spoke harsh words. His independence and spontaneous holy man's ways not sitting well with brahminic decorum, Govind soon left home.

It took some time for Govind to get settled. The government at Sorpur, some say, remained jealous of Govind' influence and kept harassing him. We hear of his stopping at several small places in the region, only to leave again soon under pressure from local authorities. Indeed, the first time Govind stopped at the present site of his shrine, which was then accessible only through thick jungle, he was pursued and driven away. Whether or not Govind really was subject to organized political harassment, in the early years of his spiritual life he may well have been outspoken and difficult to live with—his new sant path not well integrated with his brahmin background. In any event, he is portrayed during his wanderings as a charismatic holy man pitted against the local religio-political establishment—which included brahmin priests as well as Muslim administrators. He would finally be allowed to settle only at the most isolated of the sites he had found.

ii. From Holy Man to Singular Personality

The hagiographical accounts of Govind after he had settled at the site that now bears his name reveal him in a different guise. From a holy man struggling against the combined political weight of

Hindu and Islamic orthodoxies, Govind turns into a singular personality for the local Hindu community, a particularly divine individual to whom the Hindus of the area could point with honor as one of their own. No longer a wandering, struggling sādhū, Govind appears as a stable focus of divine power—a beneficient being housed at a temple complex who can present his devotees with miracles of both individual and communal import. For Govind's miracles not only resolved conflicts between personal salvation and traditional duties but also gave the group of devotees status among local Hindus—and perhaps, too, among some local Muslims.

Indeed, the first really superhuman miracle attributed to Govind during this period of his life makes the area of the shrine an immediate physical substitute for Ayodhyā, the regional Hindu temple town. At first, they say, Govind had simply recounted his experiences on the spiritual path, expounding them, as gurus do, for devotees' benefit in meditation and moral life. But one day, a devotee of Govind's came to him troubled: the devotee would have to go with his family to Ayodhyā to celebrate the feast day of Lord Rām and thus miss his guru's holy words. Noting that this might be a problem for many of his devotees from orthodox families—who traditionally went to bathe at the Saryū at Ayodhyā for the holiday—Govind proposed a solution. "If the Saryū came here," he asked, "would you still want to go to Ayodhyā?" People wondered what Govind meant by this proposal, thinking that this time their guru might in fact have overestimated his psychic powers. Yet on the feast day, we are told, a branch of the Saryū really did change its course, remaining in its new form even today as a small river near the shrine.[19] With the guru now residing near "a branch of the Saryū" a visit to him could be seen to yield some of the same type of spiritual benefit that comes from visiting a traditional holy place. Govind, the brahmin turned sant, had regained a place in the Hindu heritage: but instead of a learned officiant, he had become an object of popular pilgrimage.

In this role, Govind appears as a particularly beneficient personality. Someone who could make a river change its course could also certainly fulfill his devotees' heartfelt supplications. He gave a son to a childless merchant couple from Balliā, to the east of the region. He had told the couple to keep the source of their blessing a secret; but they couldn't, and Govind's fame as miracle-worker spread in their community, which is still well represented among the adherents of the shrine. So when another mechant was caught in a storm, his well-laden ship running dangerously low in the water, he prayed to Govind, who appeared to him in the lightning. If he were saved with his goods, the merchant promised, he would build a temple and artificial lake for the great personage. The merchant survived, made his sale, and fulfilled his vow.[20] No longer simply an enlightened holy man showing a path to salvation, Govind—now housed in an impressive temple compound—began to give boons like a deity.

Govind, moreover, is portrayed as a distinctly Hindu personality, whose pure vegetarian ways outshine those of contemporary Muslim holy men. Of these, the most illustrious in the area seems to have been a faqīr named Makdūm, with whom Govind is portrayed as being on terms of friendly rivalry. Makdūm, we are told, once tried to test Govind's vegetarian punctiliousness. Following the Muslim custom, he sacrificed a goat and had it sent to Govind: what would the famous Govind do on receiving this dubious honor? Hindu gurus, when receiving food offerings from devotees, very commonly take a small amount and then return the rest. Govind adapted this custom, merely touching the covered offering with his stick before sending it back to its giver. When Makdūm opened up the package, instead of rotting meat, he saw flowers, cloth, sugar cane, and *khichṛī*.[21] Makdūm, humbled, then sent the gifts back to Govind—this time as a sincere offering. Govind again touched the package with his stick and returned it, now turning it to gold and silver rupees. Witnessing these miracles, Makdūm finally recognized Govind's greater power.[22]

This legendary interchange between Govind and Makdūm during their lifetimes is cited to account for the distinctive traditional offerings of *khichṛī* and sugar cane at Govind Sāhib's shrine in addition to the usual ones of cloth and money; but the relationship between the shrines of the two great personages also has definite socio-economic import. At Makdūm's grave there is a month-long fair that ends just before Govind's begins. Most of the traders at Makdūm's fair simply move their goods to Govind's. Thus, as institutions, the fairs play a complementary, if limited, role in the regional economy, keeping traders busy over a substantial period of time, and fostering traffic between two local centers that serve different religious communities. To devotees, moreover, the relationship between the fairs has a hidden significance. For even Makdūm himself is said to have given utterance to what seems to some Indians to be an obvious truth: the less important person holds his court before the more important one does.[23] And Govind Sāhib's fair is clearly the larger of the two.

iii. The Heritage of the Shrine

Increasingly, the shrine and the fair overshadowed the figure of Govind as a legendary personality. Indeed, the high points of Govind's spiritual presence on earth became encapsulated in the timing of the fair, which begins in the bright half of the Hindu lunar month of Mārgaśīrṣa, starting on the tenth day. In Hindu tradition the days of the lunar cycle have their own significance, irrespective of the month in which they fall. And not only was Govind said to have been born and to have achieved his own inner realization on a tenth day in the cycle, it was also on a tenth day that he would, in his later years, give his devotees blessings. For so many devotees had begun to crowd around Govind toward the end of his life that in order to find peace enough to meditate the guru would have to retreat inside his temple, sitting in samādhi for months on end. During these periods, every tenth-day Govind would emerge to greet his disciples and give them blessings.[24] It may be this meaning of the tenth-day in Govind's life that remains more than any of the others in the scheduling of the fair—the tenth as a time when the spiritual power of Govind Sāhib flows in strength to devotees.

In addition to its manifestation in the shrine, Govind's continuing power was embodied in at least twelve disciples still remembered as gurus in the lineage. A few of these disciples produced some sant verse that is still preserved, but most are recalled primarily through memorial tombs at the places where they are said to have flourished.[25] When Govind passed on in 1822,[26] his remains were laid to rest in the temple at the shrine, which has been tended over the generations by a lineage of his successors. To which of Govind's disciples did it pass? Not to Palṭū, the most important. About the same age as his guru, perhaps even predeceasing him, Palṭū had already found a place for himself at Ayodhyā. Just as important from the perspective of the shrine's later socio-religious role, Palṭū was from a merchant caste, and the guardians of Govind's shrine were all, like Govind, to be born brahmins. Indeed, in surveying the history of the shrine, we see that to the extent the shrine as a religious institution becomes part of the heritage of the local brahmins, the guru's image as a vital spiritual personality loses its importance.

The brahminization of the shrine was gradual, and the image of a strong guru remains with Benī, the first of Govind's successors there. Benī appears both as an ardent defender of his guru and his guru's tomb and as a potent holy man in his own right, who through his spiritual power managed to secure for the shrine regular state patronage. Particularly fit for the role of guardian, Benī—though born a brahmin—was said to be skilled in sword play, always girded up and ready in case of danger.[27] His spiritual prowess was revealed after his guru's death in an incident that presages the role the shrine would play in bringing together ideas of brahminic prerogative with the sant's popular power. The authorities of Tighrā, a princely state in the same region as the shrine, were troubled by a *brahm*, that is, a brahmin who had become a wandering ghost. They called on Benī to drive the *brahm* away. When Benī uttered a *mantra* to exorcise the *brahm*, the troubled brahmin ghost appeared with its complaint: in a past life the present king had done a grave injustice to him. Benī was sympathetic, but had already uttered his *mantra*, which would have to bear fruit. The two struck a bargain: the *brahm* would agree to stop bothering the court if Benī released him from the ghost's body. Satisfied with the results, the Tighrā administration began to make offerings daily during the two weeks of Govind's fair. The patronage of the shrine by the princely house of Tighrā continues, though not as munificently as before. From gold coins, the offerings became silver rupees, and finally turned into the conventional offering of *khichṛī*.[28]

In comparison to Benī's fairly short but memorable career as guru at Govind Sāhib, that of his successor, Dayāl, seems long and uneventful. In the ten years that Benī tended the shrine, he managed to continue the tradition of the site as the abode of a charismatic holy man. Dayāl, by contrast, during his sixty years as guru, "established the everyday routine"[29] by which sādhūs could live at the shrine. The details that come down to us about Dayāl present him as an established guru at an important local shrine, set in his ways, and not particularly vital. He kept a special deerskin to sit on for meditation and ceremonial, and subsisted primarily on milk—a nutrient highly favored in Hindu tradition but too expensive to be the primary food of ordinary sādhūs. Instead of narrating the miraculous powers revealed by Dayāl, devotees tell instead of the hidden meanings to be found in his mundane example. Thus they say that Dayāl refused to take medicine during a serious illness: he had to endure his karma, he explained, and didn't some people who took medicine sometimes fail to get better?[30] Having come from Faizābād, in the immediate area, Dayāl seemed to derive at least as much authority from the shrine as he gave to it. And it was probably during his long tenure that the importance of the shrine itself took precedence in the eyes of devotees over that of the guru who sat there.

The popularity of the shrine as an element in the popular local heritage seemed to present too much distraction for the next two gurus to whom it was entrusted. To pursue their own spiritual practice they retreated to Kevaṭlā, a village in the same region as the shrine but at a fair distance from it. There an āśram grew up—a spiritual retreat that would house sādhūs owing allegiance to the lineage at Govind Sāhib but wanting to distance themselves from the crowds of householder-devotees at the shrine.

With the guru himself often in residence at Kevaṭlā, the shrine at Govind Sāhib came under the control of brahmin householders, who increasingly treated it as a focus in the ritual tradition that they knew and over which they had authority. If some of the income from the shrine should come into their own pockets, this was only right. For weren't brahmins to be paid for conducting the rituals that benefit good Hindus? They had made the fair into such an important event that it could be called the village Kumbha, one of the great age-old festivals at the Hindu holy cities. Surely there was no equal in the modern state of Uttar Pradesh![31] And besides, wasn't Govind himself a local brahmin, one of their own? In perpetuating the legacy of Govind Sāhib the brahmins were celebrating their own heritage. Why shouldn't they profit?

The hegemony of local brahmin householders over the shrine was broken by the last great guru at Govind Sāhib, Rām Komal Dās, who assumed authority in 1958. Rām Komal Dās had spent his formative years at Kevaṭlā, and identified with the community of sādhūs there. He saw no reason to try to turn the shrine at Govind Sāhib back into the solitary retreat it had presumably been when Govind Sāhib first lived there, but felt that the resources of the shrine could at least be husbanded to support the sādhūs. There were certainly ample justifications to support the sādhūs' claims: the land attached to the shrine was originally given to support the holy men who lived there; and people made offerings to Govind Sāhib as a great personality in the sādhūs' spiritual lineage, not as a representative of local brahmins. From the sādhūs' perspective, at least, it was clear that they should benefit from the shrine more than they had in past decades.

Rām Komal Dās' forceful character as an individual together with his titular authority as successor did allow him to make some changes at the shrine. Certainly, the new guru kept an eye to practical affairs. Taking pains to look after the traders who came to the fair[32]—who cared more about their own convenience and profit than about who collected their rents—Rām Komal Dās was able both to expand the fair's scope and to keep control of its revenues. At the same time, as the following example illustrates, he was able to present himself vividly to devotees as a successor to the spiritual power of Govind and Benī. In the days of Govind, they say, the area around the shrine used to abound in jack-fruit trees, in which everyone delighted. During Benī's reign as guru, however, some people began eating the fruit as soon as it grew on the stalk, before it had a chance to ripen. Benī issued a warning: if people didn't stop greedily eating the fruit before it was ripe, dire results will follow. Benī's warnings remained unheeded, and the jackfruit-trees withered away. When Rām Komal Dās heard the story, he decided that Benī's curse had served its purpose and that the site should be restored to the abundance of Govind's day. "Let jackfruit-trees be planted again," he decreed. One tree was planted, but didn't bear fruit. Then Rām Komal Dās decided to put his words into action by marking with a spade the place in the earth where the tree was to be planted. This act proved efficacious, and the tree bore one fruit the first year, two fruits the second, and three fruits the third, eventually becoming a fully productive tree.[33]

As a miracle oriented around the scenery at a place, the story of Rām Komal Dās and the jackfruit trees presents Govind Sāhib as a shrine in a local heritage. At the same time, the story demonstrates some dynamics of authority in institutions that continue the legacy of a singular personality. Rām Komal Dās, while presiding as hierarch, can consciously change the policy of a guru of the past, yet the change takes effect gradually—over the several years that the trees take to blossom. Furthermore, putting the change into effect demands actions, however symbolic, in addition to words: Rām Komal Dās himself has to mark the earth with a spade. Yet while the story tells of active, powerful gurus and disobedient devotees, it shows us no sādhūs in quiet meditation. Commanding and forceful, in control of his office, Rām Komal Dās as we see him here does not present an image of an enigmatic holy man. But these, too, have been produced by the lineage over the past decades, flourishing at the āśram at Kevaṭlā.

b. Holy Men at Kevaṭlā

The name over the gates of the hermitage at Kevaṭlā presents it as an establishment dedicated to different ends than the complex at Govind Sāhib. Not a popular shrine identified with a past guru, this is the Govind Gyān Yogāśram—a retreat (*āśram*) in which to practice yoga and acquire divine wisdom (*gyān* = Sanskrit *jñāna*). While the āśram compound contains some graves of its past gurus, modestly kept up and revered by the people who live there, it does not feature tall spires or artificial pools like those at Govind Sāhib. Located eight miles in from the main road, the āśram at Kevaṭlā is neither easily accessible to casual devotees nor meant to attract them. It is instead a place that committed renunciates make their home, with between ten and twenty sādhūs regularly in residence. Tending fields and livestock attached to the āśram in addition to carrying on study and meditation, the sādhūs at Kevaṭlā manage to maintain a fairly independent communal existence.

Like the shrine at Govind Sāhib, the āśram at Kevaṭlā evolved from the retreat of a solitary sādhū. But the founders of the two lineage centers arrived under different circumstances, which presaged the different directions in which the institutions developed. Govind, we recall, was said to have come to the site of his shrine in order to flee the wrath of his persecutors, an influential preacher held suspect by political and religious authorities. Arriving at his secluded spot through necessity, not choice, Govind Sāhib did not discourage admirers—whose visits increased with his fame. The founder of Kevaṭlā, on the other hand, a disciple of Dayāl's named Jītā Dās, came from the shrine at Govind Sāhib after it had become well established as a local religious center. More a contemplative sādhū than a popular preacher, Jītā Dās is represented as having fled the crowds at the shrine to pursue his meditation in private. Inheriting the mahantship at Govind Sāhib from Dayāl, Jītā Dās nevertheless continued to live most of the time at Kevaṭlā. The two sites have thus remained closely connected: Kevaṭlā spoken of as under the authority of Govind Sāhib, the older and larger center, while Kevaṭlā has often housed the joint spiritual head of both places.

The growth of the āśram at Kevaṭlā was presided over by two

sādhūs who followed Jītā Dās: Sītārām Dās, the appointed successor, gave the place spiritual authority; Jangī Dās, who arrived later on the scene, gave it vital personal energy. The titular head of both Govind Sāhib and Kevaṭlā, Sītārām Dās seems to have been by nature a recluse, like Jītā Dās living alone in a hut by the Saryū. He thus delegated authority for practical affairs at Kevaṭlā as well as Govind Sāhib. While Sītārām Dās retained the title of mahant, Jangī Dās—who was entrusted with the day-to-day running of Kevaṭlā—was called *adhikārī*, "the one in charge" and gained stature as an important guru in his own right. As holy men, the three most notable gurus at Kevaṭlā had their own styles of dealing with devotees and managing institutions.

i. The Ways of Holy Men

A pioneer, a recluse, and an active sādhū, Jītā Dās, Sītārām Dās, and Jangī Dās are remembered as distinct individuals; nevertheless, as a group all three present images that differ from those of the first gurus at Govind Sāhib. Closer in time than Govind and Benī, the Kevaṭlā gurus are remembered as human persons, not wondrous beings who could accomplish superhuman feats. But in contrast to Dayāl, presented as teacher and maintainer of Govind Sāhib's shrine, the Kevaṭlā gurus could perform minor miracles, or at least have esoteric experiences. Neither legendary personalities nor exemplary hierophants, they are presented as holy men, fathoming the ways of the wise and revealing their hidden powers to devotees.

Of the three great gurus at Kevaṭlā, Sītārām Dās seems to have left the least striking impression. Idealized as a learned ascetic, remote and preoccupied, he may not in fact have interacted much with devotees. He ate only once a day, they say, for the most part greens and squashes he grew himself near his hut.[34] Reportedly a student of Sanskrit who knew the Gītā by heart and recited from it daily, he is said as well to have bathed daily in Saryū and performed ritual prayers. Sītārām Dās is described as a solitary figure who wore a necklace of tulsī beads, sat in his straw hut by the Saryū and chanted the name of Rām.[35] In this idealized traditional picture of Sītārām Dās, his career as a sādhū represents a steady progression toward spiritual aloofness, a treading of the pristine path of inner renunciation that is held out as the common goal of sādhūs. A native of the nearby town, he came to his guru as a child and received his education at Kevaṭlā. A loyal disciple, he duly inherited his guru's authority. But like many sādhūs whose daily needs are met, he was not particularly interested in expanding his circle of disciples. Only unwillingly, they say, did Sītārām Dās take on the burden of being mahant, and he was glad to be able to dispense with the practical responsibilities of his office. Never moving too far from the physical place of his birth, he seemed instead, through daily methodical practice, to have moved steadily within. Any mysteries he knew and spiritual idiosyncrasies he had were not for all to see; more than most of the other gurus whose careers we will review, Sītārām Dās appears less an authoritative holy man to whom others looked for salvation than an ordinary sādhū seeking his own spiritual goals.

Jītā Dās was a more memorable figure. As a popular holy man, he seems to have outshone not only his disciple Sītārām Dās but also his guru Dayāl. Dayāl, we recall, in rejecting medical treatment was able to share the wisdom of his experience with devotees, offering what he thought was sensible counsel. Jīta Dās, by contrast, could effect cures in others, and in interacting with disciples is famous not for sensible advice but for enigmatic utterance. We are thus told of one of Jītā Dās' sick devotees, who dreamed that the saddle of the camel on which his guru used to ride had broken, which in fact it had. The devotee then ordered his servant to stop treating him in order to take the devotee's own saddle to the guru at Kevaṭlā. The sick man immediately got well, but not before Jītā Dās, receiving the saddle, asked the servant: "Does your master have samādhi just like a guru?"[36] Through his cryptic statements Jītā Dās could not only exercise his spiritual power, but also hint at his spiritual state. He admonished a devotee who had given him some of his favorite kind of bread but had served it too hot: "You shouldn't ever serve (me) anything that's so hot; it makes God's mouth burn."[37] Was Jītā Dās himself to be taken as a physical embodiment of the divine? Or was he so attuned to the Lord that his distress caused corresponding distress to God? Perhaps these were questions he wanted the disciples who interacted with him to ponder.

Provoking devotees in everyday life and adorning their existences with extraordinary events, Jītā Dās as living holy man presents a figure offering marked contrasts to Govind conceived as singular personality. Jītā Dās projects his divine presence unexpectedly into people's lives—intimately, through their sleep and their service to him—in ways they do not particularly seek. The unusual events that occur in his wake may be understood, at least by the outsider, less as inexplicable miracles than as coincidence, perspective, and psychological suggestion: the vision of the camel-saddle and spontaneous cure; puzzling warnings about the mouth of God. Perceived subjectively by devotees, his is a hidden divine presence known only to the wise. By contrast, when Govind brings the Saryū down from Ayodhyā, he is seen to have performed a concrete physical miracle on a grand scale. His more mundane miracles, moreover, appear as simple boons: he grants gifts of children and protection from harm when asked, without personal lessons attached. He is a superhuman fount of grace and power, not, like Jītā Dās, an enigmatic divine presence.

Where Jītā Dās is portrayed as the commanding, somewhat perplexing guru, receiving gifts and service, Jangī Dās—the person "in charge" who built up Kevaṭlā—is presented as a resourceful and energetic devotee, quick to serve the needs of sādhūs. His name derives from a word meaning "battle" and even as an old man of ninety, they say, he was called "valiant in battle" by a respected guru. The guru, distributing raw sugar at a feast attended by Jangī Dās, became visibly annoyed at the slowness of his assistant, who was bringing the sugar piece by piece from a bowl several yards distant. "Is this the way to welcome sants?" shouted the venerable host. Acting immediately on the guru's explicit revealed wishes, Jangī Dās lifted up the whole heavy bowl of raw sugar and brought it to him. The guru, involved in his distribution, hadn't noticed what Jangī Dās had done and at first thought that Hanumān—the mighty monkey god, Ram's faithful servant—must have moved the bowl.[38]

Earlier, Jangī Dās had employed his prodigious energy at Kevaṭlā. The place was extremely run down when he arrived there—a sādhū about thirty, sometime in the middle of the first decade of the present century. One of the doors had broken on the memorial temple to Jītā that Sītārām Dās had commissioned. But the temple was barely functional anyway, open only in the evening, when a householder brahmin came to do pūjā. Even the simplest provisions were not always available at Kevaṭlā, and Jangī Dās, they say, sometimes had to exist on water alone. From these very modest beginnings Jangī Dās turned the site into an āśram for sādhūs to inhabit, constructing buildings and putting fields under cultivation. Himself an imposing presence, a big man bearing the marks of an ascetic—matted hair, necklaces, and a marked forehead—he drew sādhūs to Kevaṭlā "not only from the Gulāl *panth* but also from the Kabīr *panth* and other sectarian lineages."[39]

While Jangī Dās built Kevaṭlā into an institution that eventually spread beyond narrow sectarian roots, his own spiritual origins pose a problem to Gulālpanthī lineage traditions. For even though Jangī Dās built the āśram around Jītā Dās' grave, he never knew Jītā as a living guru. In his natal village, moreover, he had already had a guru, still recalled respectfully in our sectarian history. Obviously, Jangī Dās remembered this guru and never disowned him. Later tradition had somehow to forge an explicit link between Jangī and earlier gurus in their succession. Thus, though Jangī Dās had admittedly experienced no physical initiation from Jītā he was understood to have made contact with Jītā in the subtle worlds and been clearly called by him to his role.

Toward the beginning of his stay at Kevaṭlā, they say, when things were at their worst and he had thoughts of leaving, Jangī Dās had a dream. Someone stood before him, short and fair, with a cap covering his ears; this being encouraged Jangī Dās to take care of the place—that was his true duty. Jangī Dās wasn't quite sure of the identity of the being he saw, but the dream was obviously a sign from above and he perservered. Five years later, when Jangī Dās finally saw a picture of Jītā Dās, he recognized him as the being who had appeared to him in the dream, short and fair with a cap covering his ears.[40] If Jangī Dās, because of his earlier guru, was never quite regarded by all as a completely legitimate member of the lineage, he had at least been authorized by the acknowledged founder of the Kevaṭlā āśram to rebuild the site.

Nevertheless, vital traditions with strong lineage identities are not likely to tolerate an outsider in their midst easily, so Jangī Dās' resounding success at Kevaṭlā speaks not only about *his* personal attainments but also about the condition of the Gulālpanthī sādhūs at the time of his arrival. Sādhūs looking at the lineage from within may well have seen a need for some spiritual revitalization. In his sectarian history, Prabhū Dās describes Jangī's guru, Raghuvīr Dās, as "a practitioner of *surat śabd* yoga"[41]—a type of yoga that Prabhū Dās has characterized in conversation as known to the early gurus of the lineage but not to him personally. Less worried about the purity of their lineage than its extinction, the sādhūs may have realized the value of new spiritual sources from wherever they came. At the same time, the sādhūs' acceptance of Jangī suggests that socioreligious force of lineage identity need not be narrowly limiting: sādhūs could recognize their kinship with ascetics from other traditions as well as with householders from their own. The picture we get of Kevaṭlā, then, is as a place for sādhūs—primarily Gulālpanthī but not exclusively so—and dedicated to sādhūs' interests.

ii. The Sādhūs and the Shrine

If the sādhūs had a center of their own, why were they so concerned about the disposition of Govind's shrine at all? To be sure, there were the personal rivalries bound to surface within a fairly ingrown and provincial community, where most of the members had known each other for decades. And there was the obvious matter that the Kevaṭlā sādhūs were traditionally subordinate to the mahant at Govind Sāhib, so that a forceful guru there could affect them strongly for good or ill in many practical ways. Yet it was not only the Kevaṭlā sādhūs who were involved in the dispute, but those attached to other Gulālpanthī centers throughout the region, small and large. And for these the results of the succession dispute at Govind Sāhib was less a matter of immediate practical concern than one of broad symbolic value.

The success of the annual fair at Govind Sāhib made the economic stakes offered by the shrine obvious to everyone involved, and these were spoken about frankly. Since the mahant was seen as the "owner" of the shrine, he was entitled to the receipts and could dispose of them as he liked. A vigorous guru acting in the sādhūs' interests would put the proceeds of the fair back into the shrine, making it a comfortable place for sādhūs to live. There was no need—indeed, no way—to turn the shrine at Govind Sāhib into another Kevaṭlā; but the fields at Kevaṭlā couldn't support everyone, and except for the days of the fair the shrine complex was a big enough place for a moderately sociable sādhū to be content. Let the material wealth that comes from the grace of Govind serve his sādhūs. Weren't their motives higher than those of brahmin householders? Moreover, didn't the sādhūs as a group have the interests of the shrine at heart? Who knows what individual householders, with their different worldly concerns, would do with the proceeds if they had control of them? These were the sentiments voiced by the sādhūs while the succession dispute was in progress.

But the idea that the guru in fact possesses the shrine led beyond issues of simple economics to the strength and nature of lineage institutions. There was, first of all, the question of the collective authority of the Gulālpanthī mahants scattered through eastern Uttar Pradesh. They had consecrated the sādhūs' candidate;

what right had these local people to put forward their own? Wasn't the shrine primarily a center in their common lineage? Most of the mahants were themselves sādhūs—the only important family line of succession being among *kṣatriyas* at Chitbaṛāgāon, who owed their status to their descent from a sant, not a brahmin. So there were few among the mahants to have a particular interest in the cause of the householder-brahmins around Govind Sāhib. Moreover, the communal sentiments and socio-religious interests of most mahants were against the householders' position in principle. After all, the prime qualification of the householders' candidate was that he was, like the householders, a brahmin. And although there were a number of brahmin sādhūs who had attained positions of influence, most of the sādhūs came from clean farming castes. The preponderance of the number of sādhūs from lower castes in the *panth* was no doubt due in part just to its origins in a heterodox sant lineage. Certainly, it was fine for the *panth* to adopt some customary rituals and proven ways of meditation practice derived from the Hindu heritage. But there was no need for it to accede to brahminic authority.

The conflict between competing bases of religious authority at Govind Sāhib found visible ritual expression in the identity of the *pūjārī*, the officiant who performed the regular worship at Govind's tomb—which is itself a phenomenon needing some explanation. While immediate disciples of recently deceased gurus are likely to continue to invoke their gurus' grace, Hindus do not regularly worship holy men of past generations, who are seen to pass their spiritual power to chosen disciples. Thus, within the Hindu heritage, the performance of regular ritual worship to a past guru, as to a god, marks his transformation into a singular personality: a being beyond ordinary holy men, who continues to grant blessings to devotees who approach him at his shrine. As at the shrines of most Hindu deities, ritual worship, once instituted, needs to be maintained regularly; otherwise the deity may leave—or worse—become angry. One of the main responsibilities of the mahant, therefore, is to make sure that the ritual worship is performed. But mahants may be busy men, not always able to find the time for the worship, which is preferably performed at least twice daily, at dawn and dusk. When the mahant is involved in other spiritual or mundane affairs, or is away on tour, he may delegate the performance of the ritual to someone else. The question at Govind Sāhib has been to whom: a householder brahmin or a sādhū?

Historical sources allow us only to conjecture about the origins of ritual worship at Govind Sāhib, but memories of the more recent past can suggest how it developed. Whether or not Benī had instituted ritual worship to Govind—his own guru—regular ceremonial had probably begun by Dayāl's time: we recall how Dayāl's disciple Jītā Dās had left Govind Sāhib because of the crowds at the shrine. Dayāl may well have had brahmin *pūjārīs* to help him with the ritual, but he was also himself remembered as a strong presence. Whoever performed the worship at Govind Sāhib, there was still a living mahant there who embodied the sant's spiritual lineage. Jītā Dās, also remembered as a strong personality, even when living at Kevaṭlā came regularly to Govind Sāhib at the time of the fair.[42] The situation took a definitive change, however, with the long reign of Sītārām Dās, the retiring sādhū in retreat at Kevaṭlā. During this period, the visible presence of the sādhūs at Govind Sāhib is remembered to have receded considerably: even at Kevaṭlā, we recall, before the arrival of Jangī Dās, Sītārām Dās had been content to let a brahmin householder perform the regular worship; why should he try to interfere at Govind Sāhib, miles away? When Rām Komal Dās established his authority at Govind Sāhib, one of his most significant acts was to institute sādhūs as *pūjārīs*.

Restoring the religious authority of the sādhūs at Govind Sāhib made two statements about Govind Sāhib as a singular personality, a source of grace to those who seek him. First, by instituting Gulālpanthī sādhūs as the performers of ritual worship, Rām Komal Dās highlighted Govind Sāhib's uniqueness. He was not one of the many disincarnate deities to be found within the Hindu heritage nor even a great brahmin sage of the recent past. One would expect worship to these beings to be carried out by brahmin householders. Govind Sāhib was, instead, a particular being who left a spiritual lineage of his own. His ritual worship could thus not be offered by just any brahmin. Second, the fact that the specific persons offering worship were sādhūs, archetypal holy men, indicates something about the way Govind Sāhib's grace is manifested in the world. Govind Sāhib was himself a holy man in his day, and the power at his shrine may be continually renewed by the presence of other holy men there. It will be to the benefit of all to encourage sādhūs to live at the shrine. For may not Govind's grace someday appear through one of them? Through the institution of sādhū *pūjārīs*, Govind Sāhib the focus of the local brahminic heritage now appeared as a more distinctive personality who highlighted the authority of particular holy men.

Though some brahmins suffered economic loss through the advent of a sādhū *pūjārī*, the local brahmin community was for the most part able to live with the situation religiously during the reign of Rām Komal Dās, and continued to frequent the shrine. After all, Rām Komal Dās was still a brahmin, acceptable as such, and it was he who was ultimately responsible for the ritual. The new religious crisis that arose in the succession dispute was that the candidate proposed by the sādhūs was not also a brahmin. The brahmin householders no longer saw the lineage of Govind Sāhib embodied in one of their own; perhaps more important, their sensibilities were offended at the idea of a middle-caste mahant degrading the worship of their patron sant. The sādhūs, on the other hand, had another criterion for spiritual leadership: the best of the holy men should rule. The lines of division between the parties to the conflict were well drawn. Why then did Prabhū Dās, mahant of Ayodhyā and historian of the tradition, dissent from the sādhūs' side?

c. The Heritage of Ayodhyā

The Palṭū Akhāṛā, over which Prabhū Dās reigns, is situated in Ayodhyā, the site of an old center of commerce and seat of political authority identified since the first centuries of the current era with Lord Rām's legendary capital. Located at a bend in the river Saryū, the city provides ample space for pious Hindus to perform ritual ablutions. It was thus long a pilgrimage site for Hindus of different persuasions, Śaiva as well as Vaiṣṇava. The modern temple town oriented almost exclusively toward the worship of Rām emerged only in the mid-eighteenth century, with the removal of the regional seat of Mughal power from Ayodhyā to the new capital of Faizābād. Now appearing as a more congenial place for Hindu religious enthusiasts to settle, the seat of Rām's rule naturally began to attract his devotees, whose numbers grew with the burgeoning popularity of Tulsī Dās' magnificent Hindi version of the Rāmāyaṇa. The city soon became a vital center for Ramaite sectarian teachers.[43] Palṭū lived through the transformation of Ayodhyā from bustling capital and pilgrimage place to quiet temple town and—in his attacks against orthodox hypocrisy—may have had a vision of the quarrelling sects of earlier days in mind at least as much as the tamer and more homogeneous Rām devotion of later days.

While Palṭū himself maintained a staunch independence from the ways of Rām devotion that developed at Ayodhyā, his successors at the Akhāṛā eventually adopted some of the conventional Hindu traditions that flourished there. In contrast to Krishna, playful and sensuous—a divinity beyond human constraints—Rām is portrayed as the paragon of Hindu virtues, whose behavior exemplifies pristine ideals. Thus, more than devotion to any other of the great Hindu personalities, devotion to Rām implies respect for and adherence to the precepts of the ancient heritage of the Hindus. Though there emerged forms of worship that had cultivated the sweet presence of Rām in the inward imagination, these never flourished to the extent of their Krishnaite models.[44] Instead, devotion to Rām is more often accompanied by serious acceptance of the family and caste obligations recognized by pious Hindus. An English graffito scrawled on Ayodhyā's Lakṣmaṇ ghāṭ in 1980 sums up this sentiment nicely: "Life is a duty. Please perform it." Thus, as Rām's city, Ayodhyā is literally pervaded by a reverence for the virtues of the Hindu heritage that he embodies—virtues that the successors to Palṭū's seat at Ayodhyā found it difficult entirely to escape.

i. *Family Loyalties, Ritual Worship, and Brahminical Learning*

The mahants at the Palṭū Akhāṛā have presented a continuing ambivalence toward conventional Hindu ways. Their religious authority grounded in the person of a great iconoclastic sant, the mahants never fully embraced the whole of the Hindu heritage around them. Yet most have visibly embraced one or another value rooted in the heritage of traditional Hinduism: family duties, ritual worship—even Sanskrit studies. Indeed, each of these aspects of the heritage seemed to have exercised its influence on the lineage in turn. The earliest successors to Palṭū are remembered to have come to power through the strength of family ties. Later, as celibate sādhūs became established in the succession, the Palṭū Akhāṛā was built up along the lines of an Ayodhyā temple, with a shrine to Rām and Sītā. Today, Ayodhyā serves the lineage less as a place for ritual worship than as a center of traditional learning, and some sādhūs live in the Akhāṛā for years while they pursue a course of studies at a local Sanskrit college.

It is not so much the fact that the first successors to Palṭū maintained relations with their families that stands out in sant lore, but the scandalous situations to which their familial loyalties are reported to have led. Indeed, many of the great early figures in sant tradition were themselves remembered as householders, a fact seen to resound to their credit as well as to add to their trials. In remaining householders, the early sants, as holy men, asserted their independence from the traditional Hindu path of formal renunciation; at the same time, however, family members could present obstacles to steady spiritual progress; even the great Kabīr is said to have had problems with his wife. Since the tensions entailed by family bonds may strengthen the wisdom and firmness of great-souled devotees, they are sometimes depicted as important factors in the inner lives of free-spirited and innovative popular gurus of medieval India.[45] But since the same tensions may lead lesser souls astray, throughout the world religions family ties are often routinely avoided in institutions dedicated to the cultivation of holy men: certainly the abandonment of family life is a defining feature of classical Hindu monasticism. In the lineage at the Palṭū Akhāṛā, which has developed along Hindu monastic lines, familial loyalties introduced early in the succession have been taken by later commentators as a source of spiritual corruption.

Ambivalences about family ties begin with the first successor to Palṭū at Ayodhyā, a sādhū named Palṭu Prasād, "Palṭū's Blessings." In the very act of entering the spiritual path Palṭū Prasād—who some say was Palṭū's brother or first cousin—may have been faced with more than the usual conflicts about family relationships.[46] Yet though purportedly coming to his guru through family connections, Palṭū Prasād immediately abandoned his own family on receiving spiritual initiation. More crucial to the development of the lineage, however, was Palṭū Prasād's apparently misguided respect for family affection toward the end of his reign as mahant. For the successor he appointed was the child of a woman whose own birth was due to Palṭū Prasād's intervention, a mother inordinately protective of her son.

Ḍālādāsī—for that was this woman's name—was born through Palṭū Prasād's grace to a childless brahmin couple. The guru felt responsible for her and had her given in marriage to one of his devotees. She lived at Mokalpur, a village about ten miles from Ayodhyā, where her husband tended land that had been given to his guru. Bearing three sons, Ḍālādāsi is remembered in tradition for her singlemindedness in pursuit of their prosperity. The immediate prize she sought was the succession at Ayodhyā, which would also give title to the land at Mokalpur where the family lived. She was afraid of what would happen if Lakṣmaṇ Dās, recognized as one of

Palṭū Prasād's most qualified disciples, should inherit the seat. Ḍālādāsī schemed and plotted but, on finding herself unsuccessful in her maneuvers, threw herself into a well. Her maternal devotion, however, finally did bear fruit. Palṭū Prasād, moved by this news of Ḍālādāsī, appointed her son Kisun Dās as his successor—which made Lakṣmaṇ Dās angry enough to break his ties with Ayodhyā and found a seat of his own.[47]

The story of Ḍālādāsī reveals the ways in which values idealized in an eternal heritage may appear in their darker aspects when imported into a lineage of holy men. Whatever spiritual intuitions might have been behind Palṭū Prasād's choice of a successor, his reaction to Ḍālādāsī's desperate act seems to demonstrate less an adherence to righteous duty than misplaced attachment and belated remorse. Ḍālādāsī, in her own singlemindedness and despair, takes extremes of maternal devotion too far, becoming an exemplar of a bad mother, not a good one. Indeed, the drama of Ḍālādāsī presents a curious parallel to the story of the Rāmāyaṇa continually narrated at Ayodhyā. The role of Rām's father, the imperfect sovereign, is played by Palṭū Prasād, temporarily blinded by a mistaken sense of duty to a woman to whom he had been attached. Ḍālādāsī appears in the part of that woman, Rām's step-mother, whose schemes for her own son left Rām an exile. Our story has no true hero, only a figure named after Rām's faithful brother Lakṣmaṇ—a figure who, in contrast to the Rāmāyaṇa's heroes, has lost faith in his spiritual father and brother and leaves Ayodhyā never to return. In the epic Rāmāyaṇa family disharmony and moral disorder are finally resolved with the restoration of the kingdom to its rightful heir, when political order, religious right, and family duties coalesce. No such neat conclusion is possible in the real-life situation among Palṭū's successors. For Rām needed only persistently to follow the duties prescribed by the Hindu heritage for his story to reach a satisfactory conclusion. The successors to Palṭū, on the other hand, were substituting heritage values for those of holy men, and had to find a new resolution of their own.

It took a few generations for holy men's ways to come to the fore again at Ayodhyā. Ḍālādāsī's son Kisun Dās himself is not remembered as an accomplished yogi.[48] He was married, with seven sons and three daughters, and passed the succession on to his oldest son. The latter, though apparently remaining unmarried, kept up his family responsibilities. He was, moreover, no ascetic. He supported his brothers and sisters through his income as guru and is famous for spending lavishly on his sisters' weddings. He liked pomp in his everyday affairs, too, they say, and would go to visit his devotees in a palanquin.[49] After about forty years' reign as guru he was succeeded by his younger brother, who began to restore the lineage as a tradition of ascetic yogis. Called Paramhaṃsjī, "the highest divine swan," this guru has inspired stories not only of renunciation but also of miracles: when Paramhaṃsjī heard talk of his marriage, they say, he immediately renounced the world; when workmen dumped some rice-straw on him while he was meditating, he is said to have sat under it for six months, later reporting that he regularly received food and milk.[50] All descendants of Ḍālādāsī, these three gurus seemed to have lived for the most part at Mokalpur, which was in effect the family farm. Palṭū's old samādhi at Ayodhyā had fallen into disrepair.

The site at Ayodhyā was restored by the first of the mahants who came from outside the family line of Ḍālādāsī, Triveṇī Dās. Indeed, Triveṇī Dās' work on the Akhāṛā at Ayodhyā may have been a move on his part to shift the seat of authority away from the legacy of Ḍālādāsī's descendants at Mokalpur. Nevertheless, like the descendants of Ḍālādāsī, Triveṇī Dās was a brahmin, and in refurbishing the Akhāṛā, he drew on the forms of brahminic worship appropriate to his caste status. Clearly not of the same biological lineage as his immediate gurus, perhaps he could demonstrate that he was a more punctilious brahmin than they. At any rate, by Triveṇī Dās' day at the turn of the present century Ayodhyā was indisputably a Hindu temple town, and it was almost inevitable that the Palṭū Akhāṛā would take on some of the characteristics of the institutions that surrounded it.

Nevertheless, only gradually did ritual worship to Rām and Sītā of the type found all over Ayodhyā come to prominence. According to Tapsījī, a revered Gulālpanthī sādhū who had long resided at the Akhāṛā, Triveṇī Dās had first instituted image worship at the Akhāṛā with a temple to Jagannāth, "the Lord of the World," whose most famous temple is at Puri. A deity less easily imagined in human form than Rām and Sītā, less exuberantly portrayed in mythic image and iconic convention, Jagannāth may have seemed to someone with a lineage rooted in *nirguṇ* traditions a more suitable object of worship than Rām and Sītā. In any event, worship of Jagannāth and not Rām distinguished Triveṇī Dās as an individual holy man, one ready to steer a spiritual course that differed from the path most commonly followed by the many Vaiṣṇavas around him. Still, says Tapsījī, Triveṇī Dās allowed one of his devotees to build a temple to Rām and Sītā *below* Palṭū's memorial tomb, where the Jagannāth temple was located. As long as this devotee lived, he maintained the expenses for separate ritual worship at this temple; but when he died the images were moved up to the tomb, and eventually outshone the icon of Jagannāth. The institution of ritual worship that may have started as an assertion of independence from the family legacy of Mokalpur thus ended up as the conventional form of worship at Ayodhyā.

Whatever the importance of ritual worship at the Akhāṛā in its heyday, however, its significance for the mahants did not last. When Triveṇī Dās died in 1914 at the age of fifty-five, the succession passed to Jagannāth Dās, a younger disciple of Paramhaṃsjī, their common guru. Like Triveṇī Dās, Jagannāth Dās was a brahmin, but unlike his predecessor, he was of local origins, born in Mokalpur village. His father, they say, had lost six children in succession and, fearing for the health of this one too, gave the newborn to the local guru. Inheriting the seat at age sixteen, he is said to have become absorbed in spiritual practice by the age of twenty. Jagannāth Dās was a more contemplative individual than his predecessor, devoted to yoga instead of ritual worship; he is remembered as a powerful holy man who could effect miracles.[51] Content to remain at home in Mokalpur, he built the site up into a thriving farm worked by sādhūs—an establishment that in some ways resembles Kevaṭlā.[52] During his day, Mokalpur gained fame as a place of holy men and attracted the large majority of devotees.[53] By the end of his life, however, Jagannāth Dās had retired from view, entrusting the affairs of both Mokalpur and the Palṭū Akhāṛā to the disciple who eventually became his successor.

The visible interest in scholarship found among the sādhūs at the Akhāṛā today seems to date from Jagannāth Dās' era, beginning with renewed attention to disseminating Palṭū's verses and continuing with a pursuit of Sanskrit learning. The first collection of Palṭū's verses published in the lineage came under the imprimatur of Jagannāth Dās himself,[54] and his successors at the Akhāṛā have culled the manuscripts in their collections with the aim of publishing selections of their own.[55] Prabhū Dās, moreover, the present mahant, is a Sanskrit scholar, principal of a small Sanskrit college in Ayodhyā. His occupation seems to influence a current important function of the Akhāṛā, which provides a residence not only for the mahant—whose work keeps in Ayodhyā—but also for other Gulālpanthī sādhūs who study at the college.

ii. Similar Foci in Different Configurations: The Palṭū Akhāṛā and Govind Sāhib Today

A residence for scholarly sādhūs and a place of ceremonial worship to Sītā and Rām, the Palṭū Akhāṛā is nevertheless, like Govind Sāhib, a center for the Gulālpanthī tradition—and as such continues to elevate some of the holy-man ways of the sants. Yet the relationships between holy man, singular personality, and eternal heritage at these two centers of tradition present differing configurations, which in turn lead to different tensions among groups of people affiliated to each establishment. In contrast to the struggle at Govind Sāhib, which pitted sādhūs against householders, at the Palṭū Akhāṛā tensions have emerged between different groups of sādhūs: Prabhū Dās and the students at his college on the one hand, and more ascetic, rustic, yogis on the other. In fact, in the recent past the Akhāṛā was home to one of the most illustrious ascetic yogis in Gulālpanthī tradition. Known as Tapsījī, "Respected Ascetic," this yogi lived at the Akhāṛā during the reign of the previous mahant. With the accession of Prabhū Dās, however, Trapsījī went off to live with his disciple, a sādhū who practices Ayurvedic medicine in Ayodhyā. Tapsījī's departure from the Palṭū Akhāṛā has been explained as a conflict of personalities between the old yogi and the new scholarly mahant, which was exacerbated by tensions between their different religious styles. How do these two gurus find support for their alternative styles in the particular religious legacies that had come to prominence at the Akhāṛā? And how did the relationships among those legacies differ from their counterparts at Govind Sāhib?

The contrasts between the configurations of foci that developed at the Palṭū Akhāṛā and Govind Sāhib appear particularly acute amid some obvious similarities between the two Gulālpanthī centers. Dominating at both places are figures of past sants who have been revered as singular personalities. The images left by these personalities, moreover, were nurtured in contexts featuring a version of the brahminic heritage, which has led to the establishment of brahmin mahants. But the images left by Palṭū and Govind contrast with each other; the versions of the brahminic heritage in which their shrines developed were not the same; and these differing contexts gave their own significances to the institution of brahmin mahants. Varying in different ways at the two centers, similar structural elements came into alternative relationships.

The contrast between the images left by Palṭū and Govind Sāhib is nicely illustrated in the following tale: a story of Govind's test of his discipline Palṭū that falls into a well-established genre of post-classical Indian hagiography describing disciples' trials.[56] Featuring the artificial lake at Govind Sāhib, the story presents Govind in his glory as established guru at a well-endowed dwelling-place; Palṭū, by contrast—the more striking poet of the two—triumphs through his wit. The test that Govind gave to Palṭū had two parts. First, telling Palṭū to catch him, Govind turned into a fish among many others swimming in the lake; in order to discern his guru, Palṭū turned into a heron. Then the roles in this game of hide and seek were reversed; only this time Palṭū, the one who was hiding, could not be found. For Palṭū surpassed his guru in esoteric skills by transforming himself into the lake's *water*—pervading the entire lake just as the supreme divine essence pervades the universe. In this story, told by Prabhū Dās of the Palṭū Akhāṛā, Govind is depicted as the beaming master satisfied with his disciple, but Palṭū is presented if not as wiser then at least as more clever, revealing spiritual truth in concrete terms, just as he does in his verse.

The differing images of Palṭū and Govind as singular personalities have been colored by the environment in which they lived as gurus; in establishing their paths as holy men, moreover, each had to come to terms with the heritage that he knew. Govind, a brahmin by birth and educated in Sanskrit at Banāras, after troubles with family and caste-fellows eventually found contentment as a recluse. By choice a sant, he looked to a spiritual source beyond his brahminic heritage; but he could not completely disown the tradition into which he was born. The quiet place he found was thus able to become a fresh source of grace for a local Hindu community. Commemorating a sant who was also a brahmin, the shrine at Govind Sāhib was able to dignify a popular form of piety for high-caste folk, many of whom could identify with Govind more easily as a great past personality coming from their ranks than as an eccentric living holy man. Palṭū, whose voice was to resound more loudly than Govind's throughout North India, sought the nearby pilgrimage town to proclaim his message. A Hindu by birth but no learned brahmin, Palṭū set out to challenge the heritage at its most important center in his region. Threatened, they say, by the priests of Ayodhyā, Palṭū during his lifetime probably did make his presence felt in the town as an iconoclastic holy man. Yet given what we know of his immediate successors at Ayodhyā, any impact he may have had while alive probably dissipated soon after his death. And though Palṭū's verses today are known by devotees far beyond Ayodhyā, there his message is largely forgotten.

But it was not only the dearth of qualified successors to Palṭū that has made the Akhāṛā appear less than a beacon of sant iconoclasm in Ayodhyā; the communal climate in the town may also have played a role. Even though Ayodhyā was an old Hindu pilgrimage place, by the thirteenth century it had fallen under definitive Muslim rule, and many of the natural sites that stood out to Hindus as holy also appealed to Muslims.[57] As Hindus since Palṭū's day reclaimed the sacred spots described in their old texts, they had occasion to build around forts and mosques—some of which were still in use. The rivalry between Hindus and Muslims that resulted was not like the ceremonious one-upsmanship between holy men that is suggested in the story told earlier of Govind and the Sufi Makdūm. That story, with appropriate changes, could just as well have featured two Hindus revered at not-too-distant, sometimes competing shrines—resembling in this respect the contest at the lake between Govind and Palṭū. Instead, the rivalry between Hindus and Muslims in Ayodhyā entailed persistent clashes of communal claims still visible at the site of a prominent shrine in Ayodhyā today.[58] Though such communal strife might have led Palṭū himself to question the virtue of any heritage, it could lead lesser souls to take a stand on one side or the other. And most of the people who turned to the Palṭū Akhāṛā were, like Palṭū, from Hindu castes—even if frequently from undistinguished ones. In spite of what Palṭū had said about Sanskritic orthodoxy during his own day, the Palṭū Akhāṛā in Ayodhyā was to become a center for a self-consciously Hindu community.

The Hindu self-consciousness at Ayodhyā can contribute to the prestige of a brahmin mahant there in ways not found at Govind Sāhib. A learned brahmin reigning at the Akhāṛā may appear as a focus for the Hindu high-cultural tradition, the guardian of heritage wisdom beyond the grasp of common middle-caste devotees. At Govind Sāhib, by contrast, the brahmin mahant is a representative of his constituents' own priestly community. At both places the institution of brahmin mahants is an exception from the norm in sant lineages, where the main qualifications for a successor are ideally his spiritual gifts and administrative capacities, not his caste. But at Govind Sāhib, this institution may be understood as a popular tradition of local brahmin householders, standing in contrast to the spiritual elitism of the sādhūs. At the Palṭū Akhāṛā, on the other hand, the same institution represents a Sanskritic, high-cultural elitism that—in the communal context at Ayodhyā—may be revered by householders and sādhūs both.

Leading on the one hand to Sanskritic elitism and on the other to yogic practice that has little use for books, the legacy of Palṭū at Ayodhyā appears more bifurcated in tradition than does that of Govind. For what remains of Govind in the popular imagination is largely the shrine itself, a concrete ritual focus for a figure now fairly distant and abstract. Palṭū, on the other hand, continues to live primarily in his verse: devotional, yogic, and critical of most orthodox Hindu ways. At Govind Sāhib the personality of the brahmin sant has become lost in a popular brahminic heritage; at the Palṭū Akhāṛā, by contrast, a past sant of Hindu origins inspires at once holy-man iconoclasm and pride in communal heritage—legacies cherished by separate constituencies that are liable to cut across the divisions between householders and sādhūs.

Among the Gulālpanthī sādhūs around Ayodhyā, inheritors of the two different legacies of Palṭū had taken opposing sides in the fractious sectarian struggle at Govind Sāhib. To be sure, the Sanskrit scholars revering Palṭū the good Hindu, and the meditative sādhūs respecting Palṭū the unorthodox yogi are not entirely distinct. Though by the time of the dispute most of the meditative yogis had clustered at Mokalpur and most of the scholars at the Ayodhyā Akhāṛā, the two centers are not seen as totally separate from one another—certainly not as distinct as Kevaṭlā is from Govind Sāhib itself. While the latter sites early on had separate economic bases, the sādhūs at the Akhāṛā have depended for revenue on the lands at Mokalpur, which was seen more directly than Kevaṭlā as the mahant's own property. Since Mokalpur is closer to Ayodhyā than Kevaṭlā is to Govind Sāhib, movement between shrine and farm is easier: rustic sādhūs may come to live for a while at Ayodhyā; Prabhū Dās goes to live for periods at Mokalpur, his students may accompany him, and some of them stay on. Nevertheless, as scholars studying Sanskrit at a regional pilgrimage center, Prabhū Dās and his students have a religious orientation differing from that of the more contemplative sādhūs at Mokalpur—who in caste and education fall more closely within the unexceptional mainstream of Gulālpanthī tradition.

Prabhū Dās himself is a brahmin and admittedly no yogi. If the brahminic heritage he reveres presents itself in a different form from that known to the householder brahmins at Govind Sāhib, it still highlights many of the same values. These, moreover, contrast with those of the more unorthodox Gulālpanthī holy men, at least one of whom, Tapsījī, has challenged his authority. As often occurs in matters of sectarian politics, in Prabhū Dās' alliance with the householders' candidate at Govind Sāhib religious priorities act in unison with factors of personal advancement. However the significances of the institution of brahmin mahant at Govind Sāhib and the Palṭū Akhāṛā may differ, maintaining the institution at Govind Sāhib makes Prabhū Dās' own position in tradition appear less anomalous. And in diverting power from the mainstream sādhūs—whose holymen's ways are not entirely his own—Prabhū Dās orients the tradition more clearly into the heritage that he cherishes.

As a way of preserving the traditions of his *panth*, Prabhū Dās' pursuit of orthodox Hindu learning serves contradictory ends. To the extent that Gulālpanthī tradition does become oriented toward the greater Hindu heritage, it is likely to lose its identity as a distinct *panth*. And voices among the gloomier sādhūs have predicted the demise of the *panth* "within fifty years." Should the *panth* become extinct, moreover, it would likely leave little trace, for its iconoclastic origins have provided few mythic resources that the heritage could nurture on its own terms. What the Gulāl *panth* has produced, however, is an array of holy men. Though their life stories are of interest to both devotees and scholars alike, as mortals they are likely to be quickly forgotten. And it is the biographies of these gurus that Prabhū Dās has thought to record in his history. Indeed, without Prabhū Dās, the brahmin man of letters, we would not have much of a story to tell here.

3. One Shrine, Alternative Visions

The saga of Govind Sāhib's shrine can do more than illustrate the dimensions of the immanent foci; it can also show us how to look at them as the elements of a systematic grammar, in India and beyond.

The succession struggle itself shows us vividly some ways in which the immanent foci as bases of religious authority *compete* with one another. To serious devotees, receptacles for faith are irreducible, ultimately distinct. In successful institutions, different foci often do manage to find modes of accommodation: the long chain of mahants who had been both brahmins and sādhūs were able both to present aspects of the Hindu heritage and to appear as holy men, thus offering something to groups with conflicting religious interests. Eventually, however, the separate nature of these types of authority made itself felt. When no acceptable brahmin sādhū could be found, hard choices had to be made: What did the shrine truly represent? Whose was it *really?*

Since the parties' disagreement on basic issues did not permit compromise, they resorted to the courts. No end to the litigation was in sight when I left the scene in 1981, and I do not know what resolution has been reached, if any. But the strong feelings that had been aroused were by then causing some serious disarray among the sādhūs. A few days after an adverse court decision, Tapsījī, who had had a history of high blood pressure, suddenly died of a stroke. Somber and pessimistic, important Gulālpanthī sādhūs collected for a funeral feast at Tapsījī's disciple's place in Ayodhyā, speaking openly of the problems with caste and money that their litigation presented. Prabhū Dās, whom one would have expected to find at a sādhūs' gathering in Ayodhyā, was conspicuous through his absence. He had previously scheduled a trip to visit distant devotees, we were told, and had to send his regrets. A tense confrontation was avoided.

In addition to the fact of the crucial differences among the immanent foci, the extended story of Govind Sāhib's shrine also tells us about some ways in which the foci typically combine in a greater Hindu context—one dominated by a rich and supple *heritage*. First of all, we see the ease with which heritage elements become a part of different configurations of foci. At Kevaṭlā and Govind Sāhib as well as at the Palṭū Akhāṛā some traditional Hindu ways play a visible role in establishing sectarian identity: the dress and practice of the Kevaṭlā sādhūs, the ritual worship to Govind, Sanskrit studies at Ayodhyā. The names of the prominent figures at all three centers exploit the mythic complex featured at the regional pilgrimage place: Lakṣmaṇ Dās, Sītārām Dās, Rām Komal ("Gentle Rām") Dās.[59] At the same time, Ayodhyā and Govind Sāhib show us how the heritage frequently is subordinate to a great personality, particularly in the popular imagination: if not to a great god like Rām, then to the glorified image of past gurus. Indeed, in the figure of sant Govind, fastidious Saryūpārīṇ brahmins were pleased to have a guru of the past that they could glorify as their own. Yet while the heritage may be subordinated to another focus, it is only with difficulty consciously abandoned. Thus, great iconoclastic holy men like Palṭū could stand up in opposition to the heritage, but this stance was not often taken by successors of less inner strength and independence. Moreover, when faced with a choice between the caste prerogatives of the heritage and a guru of only marginal personal charisma, most Hindus, like the brahmins at Govind Sāhib's shrine, will opt for caste.

The place where a holy man has lived, the source of a personality's grace, the site of worship according to heritage norms, Govind Sāhib's shrine during its history has been all of these—and when we left it, at least, still was. Yet the very fact that we could leave the succession dispute unresolved is itself a fact worth noting, one that shows us vividly where we will have to locate the existence of the immanent foci as theoretical categories. For in appearing to embody all the foci, the shrine itself as a physical object is itself clearly none of them. The reality of the foci themselves, then, is to be found in the conflicting visions of those for whom the shrine is an object of reverence. Thus, to understand the dynamics of relationship among the foci we must look to some uncharted depths of religious perception.

NOTES

/1/ Bhagvatī Prasād Śukla, *Bavarī-Panth ke Hindī-Kavi* (New Delhi: Arya Book Depot, 1972; Rādhākrişna Singh, *Sant Palṭū Dās aur Palṭū Panth* (New Delhi: Sūrya Prakāśan), 1966.

/2/ Prabhū Dās, *Govind Sāhab ka Sankṣipt Itihās* (Govind Sāhib, Faizābād: Manhant Śri Rām Komal Dās Sāhib, 1976).

/3/ See, for example, the seer Āruṇi in Chhandogya Upanishad 6:1.

/4/ On the Hindu nāth traditions see Daniel Gold and Ann Grodzins Gold "The Fate of the Householder Nath" *History of Religions* 24:113–32 (Nov. 1984); for a translation of lives of the Buddhist siddhas see James B. Robinson, *Buddha's Lions: The Lives of the Eighty-Four Siddhas* (Berkeley: Dharma Publishing, 1979).

/5/ For a historian's perspective see Romila Thapar, *A History of India* (Baltimore: Penguin Press, 1966), p. 266–67.

/6/ For parallels see Geoffrey Samuel, "Tibet as a Stateless Society and Some Islamic Parallels" *Journal of Asian Studies* (February 1982): 215–229,

and Peter Brown, *The Cult of the Saints* (Chicago: University of Chicago Press, 1981).
/7/ See McKim Marriott, "Hindu Transactions" in *Transaction and Meaning* (Philadelphia: Institute for the Study of Human Issues, 1976); Ronald Inden and Ralph Nicholas, *Kinship in Bengali Culture* (Chicago: University of Chicago Press, 1977).
/8/ The number is a rough estimation on my part, gleaned from my observation of attendance at major events and talks with sādhūs.
/9/ See Shukla, 88–92.
/10/ Kaftān Ganj, on the main highway between Govind Sāhib and Āzamgaṛh city.
/11/ A short selection of Govind's Hindi verses were published by the shrine authorities as *Govind Sudhā* (Govind Sāhib, Faizābād: Mahant Śrī Rām Komal Dās Sāheb, 1976). In his introduction to that volume (p. 10), Prabhū Dās reports that Govind's Sanskrit treatise, entitled *Govind Yog Bhāskar* was published in Lucknow but is now unavailable.
/12/ Prabhū Dās, p. 2, gives the saṃvat year 1782.
/13/ Their exogamous clan name (*gotra*) was Bhāradvāj.
/14/ Prahbū Dās, p. 5.
/15/ For a longer version of the story, reflecting on the significance of caste in sant tradition, see my *Lord as Guru*, pp. 90–91.
/16/ Prabhū Dās, pp. 9–10.
/17/ Shukla, p. 71.
/18/ Ibid., p. 72.
/19/ Prabhū Dās, p. 1.
/20/ Ibid., pp. 13–15.
/21/ Khichṛī is a common dish made of rice boiled with pulse.
/22/ Ibid., p. 16.
/23/ Ibid., p. 16.
/24/ Ibid., p. 15.
/25/ In addition to Palṭū at Ayodhyā, and Benī—the principal successor at Govind Sāhib—Prabhū Dās lists 10 other figures whose samādhis are remembered, together with the samādhis' location: 1. Bānke Sāhib (Ayodhyā); 2. Rāmcharaṇ Sāhib (Govind Sāhib); 3. Thān Sāhib (Chittaurā, Faizābād); 4. Ichhā Sāhib (Bastī city); 5. Kripā Sāhib (Karmā, Allāhābād); 6. Ghanśyām Sāhib (Karhā, Āzamgaṛh, with a notable annual fair); 7. Motī Sāhib (Ayodhyā); 8. Avadh Sāhib (Movārakpur, Faizābād); 9. Parāshar Sāhib (Vankaṭiyā, Āzamgaṛh); 10. Khaḍag Sāhib (Khiṛkīghāṭ, Ģazīpur). Except for Ayodhyā and Bastī, the locations of these samādhis are small towns and villages in those districts of Eastern Uttar Pradesh where the Gulāl panth has its major concentrations. Prabhū Dās tells of verses extant for the first five of these disciples; but knows of none for the last five (pp. 19–20).
/26/ The traditional date is the eleventh of the dark half of Phalgun in the samvat year 1879 (ibid., p. 20).
/27/ Ibid., p. 20.
/28/ Ibid., p. 21.
/29/ Ibid., p. 22.
/30/ Ibid., p. 23.
/31/ Ibid., p. 36.

/32/ Ibid., p. 38.
/33/ Ibid., pp. 38–39.
/34/ Shukla, p. 86.
/35/ Prabhū Dās, p. 27.
/36/ Ibid., pp. 25–26.
/37/ Ibid., p. 25.
/38/ Ibid., p. 32.
/39/ Ibid., pp. 32–33.
/40/ Ibid., pp. 30–31.
/41/ Ibid., p. 28.
/42/ Ibid., p. 24.
/43/ On the history of Ayodhyā see Hans Bakker, *Ayodhyā* (Groningen Oriental Studies, vol. 1 [Groningen: Egbert Forsten], 1986), pp. 150–53.
/44/ On inner worship of Rām see Philip Lutgendorf, "Life of a Text: Tulsi Das' *Rāmcaritmānas* in Performance" (Ph.D. dissertation, University of Chicago), pp. 505–538.
/45/ The siddha Sarāha had his wife for a guru! (Robinson, p. 43).
/46/ R.K. Singh, p. 131. But stories of Palṭū Prasād's origins are sketchy enough to suggest that he may have been a sādhū unrelated to Palṭū by birth.
/47/ Pāṇḍul Ghāṭ in Bastī District (ibid., p. 132)
/48/ R.K. Singh, p. 132, writes simply that "he was not a respected and perfected sant."
/49/ Ibid., pp. 132–33.
/50/ Ibid., p. 133.
/51/ Ibid., p. 134.
/52/ One resident sādhū reports 125 *bīgas* (about 80 acres) of farmland at Mokalpur.
/53/ Shukla, p. 85.
/54/ *Śrī Palṭū Sāhib krit Śabdāvalī* (Ayodhyā: Mahant Jagannāth Dās Jī Mahārāj), 1950.
/55/ One had been published by 1981: *Palṭū Darśan* (Ayodhyā: Śrīmān Mahant Rāmsumer Dāsjī Mahārāj), 1977.
/56/ See my *Lord as Guru*, pp. 175–179.
/57/ Bakker, p. 59.
/58/ *Śrī Rām Janma Bhūmi*, "Ram's Birthplace," is understood to be at the site of *Bāburī Masjid:* a mosque said to have been built by Bābur, the first Mughal ruler, who flourished in the first half of the sixteenth century. In March 1986 a court ruling on litigation over the site in favor of the Hindus claims led to riots between Muslims and Hindus in several North Indian cities. (I am indebted to Philip Lutgendorf for a report on these developments.)
/59/ Both the current contenders for the mahantship, moreover, have "Rām" as an element in their names.

CHAPTER 3

ELEMENTS OF A RELIGIO-HISTORICAL SYNTAX

Though the possibility of alternative visions of a single shrine makes clear the subjective roots of the immanent foci, it does not demonstrate their universality. To what extent do the issues treated in a local Indian succession struggle reflect broader psychological realities? In order to pursue this question we will have to expand our horizons beyond Govind Sāhib and Ayodhyā to other traditions within North India and beyond. Nevertheless, a question about the meaning of sant tradition for Indian devotees provides a point of departure (as well as return) for our wider explorations: what, we ask, does the emergence of the idea of sant tradition say about the capacity of human religious perception to comprehend the holy man?

The idea of a distinct religious tradition comprising both composers of sant verse and lineages of their followers has different values among different groups of devotees. In small ingrown communities like those found among Gulālpanthīs, members' primary identification is with a particular sant lineage. At the same time, people strongly identifying with a particular lineage are still likely to recognize a spiritual commonality with others included in a broader, loosely defined tradition of sants. Thus, a Gulālpanthī sādhū living in Banāras, where his small lineage maintains no residence, stays at an āśram belonging to the Kabīr *panth*—one of the largest sant groups. Both Gulālpanthīs and Kabīrpanthīs, moreover, speak respectfully of "sants." For Gulālpanthīs the term "sant" is a standard honorific, a normal term of address for a sādhū; for Banārsī Kabīrpanthīs at their own establishment, the sants as a collectivity constitute one of several recipients of homage during daily worship.[1] By contrast, the larger collectivity of sants was the only religious tradition with which many of the great sant poets—themselves the sources of later lineages—were able to identify. Though they might scorn the orthodoxies of both Hinduism and Islam, the poets often use the term "sant" with respect and invoke particular gurus by name: Kabīr, Raidās, Nāmdev, and others.

As known to these individual gurus, the idea of sant tradition can appear as an eternal heritage: the sants of the past knew an ageless truth, and their verses remain as witness to a common shared vision. Conversely, when a sant lineage elevates its founder to the status of a unique singular personality, the idea of sant tradition as heritage can easily lose its value. The inverse relationship between the idea of sant tradition and the status of the founding guru is clearly evident among the modern Radhasoamis—numerous within India and abroad, but divided in their attitude toward sant tradition.

Devotees within both of the two major divisions of Radhasoami tradition—centered at Agra and Beas—acknowledge the existence of *sant mat*, "the teachings of the sants," which by its very name suggests that all the sants preached the same particular eternal truths. The idea of *sant mat*, propagated by Tulsī Sāhib at the end of the eighteenth century, was taken up by the nineteenth-century progenitor of Radhasoami lineage, known as Soamiji. At both Agra and Beas, *sant mat* is understood to represent a practical formulation of an older sant tradition. However in Agra, Soamiji's birthplace, *sant mat* is dwarfed by the figure of Soamiji himself as singular personality. Soamiji, according to Agra devotees, began a new religious dispensation that was merely foreshadowed by the teachings of the old sants, and by this fact is himself seen to stand beyond them, a being of a higher order.[2] Thus, at the large establishments of Soami Bagh and Dayalbagh, on the outskirts of Agra, devotees see themselves following a new Radhasoami religion that they consider to be distinct from *sant mat*. By contrast, groups within the Radhasoami lineages stemming from Beas see themselves standing solidly within an age-old tradition of sants that includes Tulsī Sāhib and Soamiji alongside Palṭū and Kabīr.[3] Beas, located in the Punjab, has long drawn many of its followers—and all of its gurus—from Punjabi Sikh families. Nānak, the first guru of the Sikhs, is generally recognized to have appeared in his own days as a North Indian sant singing in much the same style as Kabīr. So the elevation of the idea of sant tradition among Beas Radhasoamis presents the Radhasoami gurus as proclaiming the same essential message as those of the first generations of Sikhs. Indeed, as the

Beas gurus have attracted Western disciples, the eternal truths of the sants' teachings have been said to be realized by sages even beyond India.[4]

Certainly, in India itself during post-classical times, the idea of a larger tradition of sants encompassing minor lineages makes good social and cultural sense. In religion as well as politics, links between individuals were modeled on the patriarchal Aryan kinship system. Indeed, the perception of a continuity between physical and subtle worlds let people use the same terms *(bindu, bīja)* for the physical seed that gives the son his father's traits as well as for the guru's spiritual seed that informs the disciple's spiritual rebirth. Not only did political and religious figures recognize lineages governing traceable relationships, they also knew genealogies of a more mythical nature that offered them means to identify with larger groups. As Indian princes recognized the importance of lineage relationships—finding cohorts and rivals in their brothers, cousin-brothers, and uncles—so disciples talked about guru-brothers and guru-uncles. And as the princes of Western India encompassed all their extended family lines within a few common clans of mythic origin, so sants saw themselves as a loose spiritual clan composed of different lineages of gurus and disciples.[5]

Yet even though social realities and cultural perceptions made a concept of sant tradition easy to conceptualize as a mythic "clan," they do not account for the emergence of sant tradition as a concept religiously crucial for some in the first place—one that could be described, in our terms, as a highly diffuse heritage. Was not the guru of whom the sants sang himself a sufficient basis of faith? Why is it that even when the guru is presented as a holy man transcending gods and ritual, he is still usually found in a context oriented toward another focus—in a *panth* looking to a personality or in a greater heritage of sant tradition? Answers to these questions seem to lie beyond an examination of specific Indian religio-cultural contexts—to be discovered, perhaps, only in some particular dynamics of human religious perception: How do the immanent foci carry meaning to those who recognize them? How do they work as symbol?

Much has been written about the power of religious symbols over the past decades. From the studies of Eliade, Ricoeur, and Victor Turner we have become aware of the capacities of symbols to reflect infinite, many-faceted realities.[6] With classical structuralism, Levi-Strauss has told of the ways in which elements of a myth present contradictions to be mediated and resolved. As objects of religious perception, the immanent foci, too, serve as specific symbols able to reflect larger realities. But the immanent foci normally appear as elements in larger configurations, and to grasp their power as symbols attention must be paid to their relationships with one another.

The immanent foci have thus been taken as the basic components of a systematic grammar of religious perception. Following a grammarian's method, we have used the foci to label a wide range of religious materials and have then studied the patterns that are in fact historically attested. Though we will eventually find principles of contrast and complementarity governing these patterns, the structure of our grammar takes little direct inspiration from the binary phonological contrasts adapted by Levi-Straus. Combining with each other in ordered ways as elements of complex configurations, the immanent foci instead demonstrate a syntactic dynamic. They ground some recurrent phenomena of the sociology of religion in the psychology of religious perception, presenting consistent relationships that shed light on both the strengths and limits of the holy man as object of faith.

1. Regular Relationships among the Immanent Foci

Using systematic comparison to explore the significance of the holy man will entail expanding the scope of our inquiry not only beyond North India but also within it. What sorts of groups shared the larger North Indian religio-cultural context seen in our investigation of the Gulāl *panth*—groups that might present alternative configurations of elements already studied? Two types are particularly noteworthy. First, there are the many sant *panths*, among which the Gulāl *panth* figures as a fairly minor one. Second, there are sectarian movements, often called *sampradāyas*, that look to one or another of the great mythic personalities of Hinduism—usually Rām or Krishna taken as an incarnation of Viṣṇu. Both sant *panths* and Vaiṣṇava *sampradāyas*, moreover, can stand in a number of attitudes to the eternal ritual heritage of Hinduism.

Of the sant *panths*, the two most important are those that invoke the names of the two most famous sants of the past: Kabīr and Dādū. And even within just these two *panths* a wide range of stances toward the Hindu tradition is evident. At the radical extreme, the Kabīrpanthīs centered at Chhatīsgaṛh, who have drawn much of their following from the large tribal population in that region, maintain a highly independent sectarian identity. Though they sometimes claim to teach "the essence of Hinduism," both their metaphysical maps and ritual practices diverge markedly from familiar Hindu conventions. The other main branch of the Kabīr *panth*, however, with allegiance to the Kabīr Chaurā in orthodox Banāras, is more recognizably within the Hindu stream. Ritual practice in this tradition is not elaborately distinct like that of the Chhatīsgaṛhīs, but spare and aniconic, possibly passing for elemental Hindu ritual. The Dādūpanthīs of Jaipur, finally, often identify themselves today not only as Hindus but also as Vaiṣṇavas, with Viṣṇu understood as the transcendent loving Lord whom Dādū knew. When queried, many Dādūpanthīs reported interfeasting at least as much with Vaiṣṇava sādhūs as with members of other sant *panths*. Thus, within the sant *panths* we can find about as many attitudes toward the Hindu heritage as we can toward the greater heritage of sants.

Of the important Vaiṣṇava sectarian traditions, those focused on Rām command decidedly smaller followings than those focused on Krishna: the figure presented by Rām, perhaps—solidly embodying the ideals of the larger Hindu heritage—does not offer as distinctly differentiated a focus for specific Hindu devotional traditions.[7] Thus, to contrast the sant *panths* with traditions clearly focused on a mythic personality we will look to the most widespread tradition of Krishna devotion in the Hindu-speaking areas—the *puṣṭimārg*, "the sustaining way." The *puṣṭimārg* was founded by Vallabha, a teacher who came from an orthodox South Indian brahmin family recently settled in Banāras. Krishna is said to have manifested himself to Vallabha in a particular sacred icon, and the *puṣṭimārg* eventually developed elaborate forms of iconic worship. Vallabha married, and his descendants inherited his spiritual authority. Although seven especially sacred images have been entrusted to the leaders of the main seven branches of the family, all of Vallabha's descendants are referred to in conversation as his *amṣa*, "parts" of him, and they preside over worship at shrines large and small. These descendants of Vallabha have propagated the *puṣṭimārg* most fruitfully in Western India, where it has found success particularly among members of mercantile castes. Unlike most sant *panths*, the *puṣṭimārg* features definite forms of image worship and a conscious acknowledgement of family lineage. But as a sectarian tradition the *puṣṭimārg* distinguishes itself from the larger Hindu heritage through the specificity of both its images and its priestly lineage.

The *puṣṭimārg*, sant *panths*, and other traditions within India and beyond demonstrate the power of complementarity inherent in the regular relationships among the immanent foci in two ways: one bearing particular relevance for the religio-historical problems elicited by the foci in *time* discussed in chapter 1, the other for the corresponding problems in *space*. *Transformations* of foci from one into another—which seem to evolve according to the complementarity of their hidden and revealed aspects—help elucidate problems of a tradition's temporal adaptation. The most frequently attested *combinations* of foci suggest specific compatabilities among the possible dimensions of the foci as *places* of divine manifestation; these combinations can then shed light on problems of making religious distinctions in space.

a. Transformations

The history of Govind Sāhib's shrine presents an extended example of transformations from one focus to another: the sant figures as a holy man, then as a singular personality, and finally lends his name to a shrine in a local heritage. The crises we have seen accompanying these transformations are not unusual among sant *panths*, though some have endured their crises better than others. Among the most successful have been the Kabīrpanthīs of Chhatīsgaṛh, who have managed to turn Kabīr into a full-fledged singular personality with a vital heritage. Kabīr, say these sectarians, was a divine being who appeared in all the four ages and composed lengthy metaphysical tracts in Hindi verse. But several other *panths* have deteriorated even more than the Gulāl *panth*, and remain today primarily as memories. What seems to distinguish a successful transformation from a breakdown of tradition is the continuing balance it keeps between the hidden and revealed aspects of the divine that it makes manifest. In a *progression*, our term for a successful transformation, the forms of religious expression available through a tradition change along with the tradition's dominant focus: as new hidden meaning is seen in a focus, the tradition develops revealed forms that reflect it adequately. In *breakdowns*, on the other hand, a serious gap occurs between the revealed forms of a tradition and the hidden ideals that these forms are supposed to represent. Neither the theoretical nor the practical forms of religious expression offered by the tradition lead any longer to a potent appreciation of the immanent divine. For a large portion of its members the tradition appears to be presenting something meaningless, or even false.

i. Progressions

In its simplest form, the progression evident in the sant *panths* shifts the focus of tradition from the charisma of the living holy man to the scriptures left by a past sant seen as a singular personality. Certainly, wide divergences appear both in the degree of elevation of a past sant to cosmic status and the distinctiveness of the heritage that evolves in his wake. Though the verses of Palṭū and other gurus in his lineage have been taken as scripture by small groups of followers, the sants themselves retain a good deal of their humanness. Indeed, many devotees are attracted to the sant just because he was of the same caste group as they. For the Kabīrpanthīs of Chhatīsgaṛh, by contrast, Kabīr is not a scathing iconoclast but a unique manifestation of the Lord, who appeared on earth as a baby in a lotus floating on a pond. To the elaboration of this mythic identity there is a corresponding elaboration of ritual tradition. Thus, while the shrine at Govind Sāhib became a focus for a common local heritage, the Kabīrpanthīs of Chhatīsgaṛh have evolved a distinctive heritage of myth and ritual of their own, featuring unfamiliar demigods and elaborate ceremonial worship of the guru.

With their origins in the utterances of outspoken iconoclasts, however, both of these variants of sant tradition differ from a religious movement like Vallabha's, which draws directly on the sanctified symbols of a previously established heritage. The whole of Hindu tradition becomes focused in Krishna, to whom access is given by Vallabha himself. The emergence of Vallabha as holy man, then, appears as the specification of a heritage, a dynamic standing in contrast to the routinization of personal charisma found in a sant *panth* (figures 6a and b). Of course, when Vallabha passed on, his commentaries on Hindu texts became scriptures in their own right. Further, special *puṣṭimārgīya* traditions of worship grew to have an identity of their own. And like the descendants of some Kabīrpanthī gurus from Chhatīsgaṛh, the descendants of Vallabha became hereditary gurus, objects of ritual worship. Thus, the figure of Vallabha as founder of a *sampradāya* can enter into the same process of routinization that takes place with the original guru in a sant *panth*.

the
eternal heritage
of Hinduism

Krishna the
singular personality
reveals the essence of the Vedas

Vallabha the
holy man
gives access to Krishna

(a) from heritage to holy man: the emergence of Vallabha

Govind the living
holy man

Govind the
singular personality
miraculously moves the Saryū river

Govind's shrine in the
eternal heritage
of Gulālpanthī ritual tradition

Kabīr the living
holy man

Kabīr the
singular personality
incarnates through the ages

the
eternal heritage
of Kabīrpanthī myth and ritual

(b) from holy man to heritage: the development of two sant panths

the
eternal heritage
of Hinduism

Krishna the
singular personality
reveals the essence of the Vedas

Vallabha the
holy man
gives access to Krishna

Vallabha the
special personage
revered through the ages

particular Hindu scriptures and practices become the
eternal heritage
of *puṣṭimārg*

(hereditary
holy men
as objects of ritual worship)

(c) the development of the pustimarg.

Figure 6.—Three Progressions

Nevertheless, the Vaiṣṇava *sampradāya* has explicit links to the greater Hindu context that the *panth* lacks. So to insiders and outsiders alike, *panths* and *sampradāyas* present different values as elements of Indian tradition (figures 6b and c).

In progressing from one dominant focus to another, a tradition brings its hidden and revealed aspects into new relationship. In general, a singular personality begins to stand out when his revealed salvational focus is given enough hidden meaning to become a profound basis for community: Kabīr, in Chhatīsgaṛhī tradition, appears from the heavens; Krishna's teachings as explained by Vallabha are understood as the real secret of the Veda. Conversely, an eternal heritage emerges as revealed communal bases gain hidden salvational value: for *puṣṭimārgīs* as well as members of sant *panths*, major communal festivals present channels of divine grace. Further examples from India and beyond will illustrate the ramifications of these dynamics between hidden and revealed in the progressive adaptation of tradition, which are outlined in figure 7.

The revelations given by a holy man, during his lifetime often seem to confuse his disciples as much as to enlighten them. (What did Jītā Dās of Kevaṭlā mean when he said that the bread he was served had burned God's mouth?) The holy man's salvational discourse and example may have little visible consistency, and his orders to the community are frequently exasperating. (Though Jītā Dās may have commanded that his bread shouldn't be too hot from the stove, he would probably have been angry if it were served to him cold and dry.) To his disciples, then, the personal idiosyncrasies of the holy man as well as his exact cosmic mission remain elusive. What draws disciples to the often tense life around the guru is the sense that his mere proximity can bring some hidden esoteric help.

Sometimes communities around the holy man get so large that the master can no longer have much individual contact with most of his disciples. The Buddha during his lifetime is said to have attracted great crowds of followers. In modern times large establishments like the Sri Aurobindo Ashram at Pondicherry and the Radhasoamis' Dayalbagh have functioned as complex institutions around living holy men. In situations like these, standardized life ways can emerge that grow to have a value of their own as a heritage. In general, such life ways feature a common adherence to a few of the holy man's publicly revealed orders that ensure the orderly running of the community: all the Buddha's collected disciples, some say, were to seek alms in the morning; Dayalbagh's first

	holy man		singular personality		eternal heritage	
	salvational basis:	communal basis:	salvational basis:	communal basis:	salvational basis:	communal basis:
	spiritual aid	personal authority	divine communication	sacred institution	ancient knowledge	ancient ways
eternal heritage	hidden: esoteric help	revealed: master's orders	hidden: saving power	revealed: sacramental tradition	hidden: esoteric wisdom	revealed: customary law
	routinized	codified	diffused	expanded	embedded in ritual	sanctified
	the routine that the master has set for his disciples is potent; following it habitually will lead to salvation		the saving power of the Lord comes through the sacramental tradition administered through his sanctified institution		the eternal heritage is reaffirmed through acceptance of the hidden salvational power of the ancient ways	
singular personality	revealed: master's discourse and example	hidden: master's mission	revealed: holy book	hidden: the elect, the true church	revealed: received myth and ritual	hidden: organic order of divine
	recorded	made cosmic	singled out	marked by experience	focused on specific elements	given new socio-religious vision
	the master's mission was a unique cosmic event; we can participate in it through pondering his discourses and emulating his example		the singular personality is reaffirmed through voluntary fellowships looking to the Lord's word		the singular personality proclaims a new but recognizable dispensation	

Figure 7.—The Hidden and Revealed in Progressions

residents were enjoined by their guru to foster "better-worldliness" through gainful employment.[8] At the same time, the hidden spiritual help offered by the holy man is in good part received through some codified practice: the Buddha's disciples practiced concentration as part of the noble eightfold path; Dayalbagh residents should ideally get up early to carry out meditation practices learned at the time of initiation. A heritage of sanctified life ways around the living holy man may thus emerge from his revealed orders to his community and his hidden salvational help.

A holy man of the past becoming elevated into a singular personality inverts this dynamic. The revelations he presents are no longer living orders vital to the growth of community; they are instead his salvational discourse and example recorded as scripture: the Pālī Canon, the Gospels. Now a factor of his cosmic identity, the spiritual help he offers is understood as a unique saving power. The new community that emerges, then, has a definite sense of the master's mission: Buddha, perfected through countless lives, came to reveal the dharma; Jesus, the son of God, died for our sins.

The transformations in a tradition already grounded in an established singular personality present analogous dynamics, but with the more stable and elaborate bases of faith that the personality typically offers. No longer cohesive only through the authority of a living person, an expanded community looking to a singular personality is centered in a sacred institution: the Buddhist *sangha*, the Christian church. This institution, moreover, is likely to offer some revealed sacramental dimension. The Theravāda Buddhist layman ritually feeds the monks of the *sangha;* the Christian reenacts the Lord's supper in a church. A heritage develops as the Lord's saving grace becomes increasingly identified with the communal, sacramental forms. This process, richly evident in Tibetan Buddhism, is classically illustrated in the evolution of the Roman Catholic church.

When a "protestant" reformer then appears on the scene, he typically stresses the opposite aspects of salvational means and communal forms. The church that administers sacraments is not what is basic, he argues, but the community of the faithful, the true hidden church. True believers need not recognize any previously accumulated heritage, for the basis of salvation is to be found in the revealed book alone: *sola scriptura*.

Innovation and reaction progress through similar dynamics in an eternal heritage. A figure in a heritage that gains the status of a singular personality normally has roots in revealed myth to which devotees have long looked for salvation: Krishna, the divine chieftain of the *Mahābhārata;* Jesus, the promised Messiah of the Jews. The singular personality then stands as the basis for a new community, one informed by the hidden divine order revered within the heritage, but an order envisioned in a way likely to conflict with the demands of brahminic or pharisaic orthodoxy. Upholders of the orthodox heritage, in reaction, will bring together the alternative aspects of the heritage. The saving ancient knowledge comes through a hidden, esoteric wisdom, they affirm, and this knowledge can be realized through following the received customs of the community, obeying the revealed law.

If, as illustrated in figure 7, the eternal heritage and the singular personality each has its own characteristic dynamic of emergence in the development of tradition, how does the holy man typically emerge? Certainly, as radical prophet he can become the special personage at the source of a new tradition, but what role arises for the authoritative holy man who accepts most of a developed heritage? First of all, he appears as a mediator of the hidden and revealed aspects of the traditions that a heritage already offers; then, playing between the two aspects of tradition, he may further increase its preserve of lore. For those seeking salvation, the holy man gives to received myths and rituals their esoteric interpretations, some of which may be remembered and repeated by later generations. For those seeking order within community, he gives conflicts in customary law their hidden resolutions, some of which may find their way into later law codes.

During times of interaction among different traditions, the holy man may arise to play a more crucial revelatory role. Here he works not out of a single accepted set of revealed traditions, but out of a grand unifying truth. Yet the one saving truth revealed in all the world's scriptures demands a correct interpretation—and this the holy man offers through his revealed discourse and example. The brotherhood of all men everywhere demands a practical focus in community—and this the holy man provides through his initiated disciples' respect for his authority. When a holy man presents a grand unifying truth, he usually reveals it in our technical sense. That is, he gives this amorphous truth some specific working dimensions through the revealed bases of faith that he characteristically offers.

The distinctive dynamic of the holy man, then, whether within

In an Eternal Heritage

salvational basis		communal basis	
revealed:	hidden:	revealed:	hidden:
received myth	esoteric	developed	organic order of
the holy man illuminates the hidden wisdom behind received myth and ritual, sometimes making innovations in them		the holy man resolves conflicts in customs through his inner vision, sometimes making lasting contributions to traditional law	

For a Unifying Truth

salvational basis		communal basis	
revealed:	hidden:	revealed:	hidden:
all scriptures	their correct interpretation	all traditions	the secret brotherhood of the wise
the holy man interprets the meaning of the world's scriptures and exemplifies their truth through his actions		the wise from all traditions recognize the master and submit to his revealed authority	

Figure 8.—The Revelatory Roles of the Holy Man

established traditions or without, is to continually make hidden truths immediate, and mundane community divine. To do this effectively, the holy man must remain at once true to his own possibly changing realizations and sensitive to his devotees' probably changing needs. And should he begin to lose touch with his hidden sources of inspiration or fail to keep communicating convincing revelations to his disciples, his perceived position as holy man is likely first to become shaky and then to break down.

ii. Breakdowns: Corruption and Collapse

When an established tradition faces a breakdown, the processes of its disintegration are usually more complex than those of the holy man's fall from his position of esteem. But as in the latter case, the basic difficulties can derive primarily from either internal or external sources. When a gap originating from within a tradition appears to emerge between its ideals and actualities, we can talk of a case of *corruption:* the revealed forms offered by the tradition seem tainted and no longer capable of giving access to the hidden divine. When a tradition does not prove adaptable to changing external conditions, we can talk of its *collapse:* potential adherents no longer see the divine in the same forms that the tradition has always offered and leave it no practical support.

Most corruption derives from the common abuses of money, sex, and power into which unregenerate man is, alas, all too apt to fall. It is, then, understandably connected with man-made religious institutions and often directly linked to the routinized charisma of holy men. From this perspective, the passing of the mahantship at Ayodhyā to Ḍālādāsī's worldly son appears as an example of corruption stemming from avarice. But the classic example of corruption in a North Indian religious tradition is perhaps found in certain sexual practices of the later *puṣṭimārgīya gosāīṃs*, as the hereditary priests of that tradition are called.

While the devotion advocated by Vallabha was of a fairly simply and straightforward variety, it began to spawn a highly elaborate heritage under his second son Vitthalnāth, who employed trained artists and musicians to evoke the mystery of Krishna's play in the physical world. Matters eventually reached the point where several of the *gosāīṃs*—who had come to their position by birth rather than by spiritual qualification—were acting the role of the amorous Krishna with selected ladies of the community. By the middle of the nineteenth century, at least, a number of the men-folk began to object. There were court cases and a famous scandal.[9]

Without necessarily passing judgment on the value of such sexual practice for those immediately involved, we can certainly surmise from the many complaints against the *gosāīṃs* that their promiscuous behavior was seen to taint their role as foci for large segments of the community. The *gosāīṃs* did not claim to be practicing tantric yoga, but to be re-enacting Krishna's play—yet in a way not attributed to any of the great early gurus in the tradition. Thus, even though the *gosāīṃs* were seen to be divine as a "part" of Vallabha, and Vallabha really did know Krishna, the *gosāīṃs* simply were not understood by many in the tradition as able to manifest Krishna's personality in such a grossly physical way.

The distance between the common *gosāīṃs* and the image of Krishna is seen when we take the *gosāīṃs* as a final ritual focus in the long *puṣṭimārgīya* progression depicted in figure 6c. Of course, merely placing the *gosāīṃ* at the end of our depicted progression does not tell us what disgruntled devotees had in mind when they complained about the *gosāīṃ's* overstepping his role. But they were probably aware—as we are, graphically, from figure 6c—that the *gosāīṃ's* charisma was clearly derived, and that the *gosāīṃ* stood several steps away from Krishna's personality.

The imitation by human beings of the gods' scandalous behavior has been a problem long discussed in Indian religious traditions.[10] And occasionally, Indian holy men who are not *tantrikas* relate sexually (in subtle and unsubtle ways) to female devotees without necessarily raising eyebrows among their own disciples.[11] But in such cases the guru is usually understood as having himself attained the status of a self-realized divinity, aware of the broader cosmic implications of his actions. The guru's disciples, whose judgments are at issue, are attracted to him personally. The *gosāīṃ*, on the other hand, is taken as a living image who serves as an institutional focus for a largely hereditary community. To be sure, his pedigree gives him a particular type of divinity in the eyes of his disciples, but not, normally, the personal enlightenment of a guru charismatic in his own right. Thus, while the office inherited by the *gosāīṃ* does give him certain prerogatives, it also demands of him conventional moral restraints—which the vast majority of *gosāīṃs* today seem most ready to accept.

While corruption within a tradition can sometimes be remedied through specific measures of reform—which eventually took effect at the Palṭū Akhāṛā as well as in the *puṣṭimārg*—the problems of a tradition's collapse are normally presented by external macrocosmic forces and may hence be much less easy to resolve. Thus, the traditions of conquered peoples in pre-modern times have sometimes faced active persecution and been brought to total collapse. While the onslaught of a modern twentieth-century secularism has not in its turn been totally destructive to most established Western traditions, it has shaken many of them to their foundations. The ritual life of a heritage is difficult to put into practice within an industrialized society, and a pluralist culture can lead to the questioning of a personality's uniqueness. And at least as important, neither heritage nor personality often appears very real to an intellect affirming the truths of scientific empiricism. While the responses to these basic challenges include a resurgent fundamentalism very visible today, the reaction of all too many Western traditions has been a stunned collapse toward a liberal, scientifically-oriented, and tenuous unifying truth: no religion offers literal verities, but all may have relative merits, and none is particularly important.

In pre-modern historical times, however, which knew few parallels to this modern secular metaphysics, a process of effective collapse has normally been into another tradition—which most often consisted, at least in part, in a moderately developed heritage. Moreover, in these cases we usually see that whatever the dominant focus in a tradition may have been, as a process of collapse begins, heritage aspects start to take the upper hand.

Thus, as traditions forming around individual sants as holy men develop heritages of their own, they tend to lose their identity with the larger sant tradition—and then to collapse into Hinduism. Today, sant *panths* exist in various states of independence and collapse: the Kabīrpanthīs of Chhatīsgaṛh stand out as a separate tradition; the Dādūpanthīs, sometimes calling themselves Vaiṣṇavas, have a less distinct sectarian identity; there is even one group, the Charandāsīs, who are further collapsed into mainstream Vaiṣṇavism, observing much the same forms of ritual as Krishna *bhaktas* all over India. Some sants as well seem to have been the source of *panths* that are no longer extant, though the sants themselves are recognized at least locally by Hindus as their own. It is, moreover, through the perception of a greater Indian heritage that the individual sants as devotional poets are accepted into the larger Indian stream. A radical holy man, then, may leave a tradition of his own, which in turn bequeaths his rarefied image to the same heritage he rejected.

The collapse of Buddhist traditions in India and China demonstrates a similar phenomenon. What remains of the collapsed tradition is not its own coherent basis but elaborated forms that can be adapted into the new. From Śākyamuni the radical teacher have come many Buddhas with their own personalities and many schools with their own ways. It is these later developments that have left their traces in India and China, both in myth—where Śākyamuni stands as one god among many—and in Vedantic and neo-Confucian philosophy.

The role of the heritage in the assimilation of collapsed traditions is further seen in the patterns of expansion of Christianity, which as a greater religious context features a singular personality. In Asia and Africa it has been the Catholics, with access to a rich heritage able to assimilate local forms, who have been able to contain distinctive regional variants of tradition within their own.[12] What *combine*, then, are usually two heritages, and it is to aspects of the significance of this phenomenon that we shall now turn.

b. Combinations

Patterns of combination among the immanent foci present two types of dynamic. First, *restrictions* operate on the possible ways in which specific foci come together in a single configuration. Second, the configurations that do frequently recur demonstrate an internal *balance*.

i. Restrictions

Elements connected with different eternal heritages can mingle freely in times of cultural interaction, and, as we have just seen, are the aspects of one religious tradition most readily assimilable by another. Developed heritages are also the natural habitat of the holy man, who may add to the preserve of their lore. And while there may certainly be tensions among different holy men as individual concentrations of spiritual power, they and their disciples frequently accept the idea, at least, of a legitimate plurality of holy men, each with his own disciples and sphere of influence. Thus, among Indian Sufis we find the concept of *vilāyat*, a distinct geographical domain that a sheikh gives to the charge of one of his qualified disciples, its mundane boundaries explicitly delimiting the extent of each disciple's spiritual scope.[13]

But someone who looks primarily to a singular personality as a basis of faith may find it considerably more difficult than it is for the disciple of the holy man to accept the legitimacy of another focus having an equal cosmic status. For the singular personality is nothing if not singular—unique, exclusive, one of a kind. The exclusive claims of the singular personality as the focus of a world religion can thus put serious restrictions on the appearance of holy men in traditions within singular-personality contexts. When these traditions do feature holy men, they do so only through a developed heritage.

Within the greater religious contexts of the world that find a focus in a singular personality we can identify specific traditions with more or with fewer eternal-heritage elements. Among Muslims, the Sunni look to a heritage of accepted usage traced back to the prophet, while the Shia look to Ali and his descendants as very special personages—often in revolutionary and chiliastic ways. Among Buddhist traditions, The Theravāda cultures certainly contain the accumulated lore and ritual of a heritage, but the Theravāda monastic life itself should ideally adhere to a strict canon understood to represent the very words of Śākyamuni Buddha himself. In Mahāyāna, however, traditions of texts and ritual practice involving a plurality of deities develop freely among monks and laypersons, and in Vajrayāna they abound. The three major forms of Christianity also differ in the degree of profusion within the heritages they have evolved: Eastern Orthodoxy, with its separate developed national churches, showing the most diverse heritage; then Roman Catholicism, with a heritage bound to a rigorous apostolic organization that traces a well-defined succession to the singular personality; and finally Western Protestantism, finding the singular personality through "scripture alone."

The distribution of the holy man in the variants of these greater singular-personality contexts reveals a direct ratio between the appearance of the holy man in a vital role and the dominance of heritage elements. Thus, while Sufis have more often than not reached accommodation with Sunni legists, they have generally been accepted much less readily by the Shia.[14] The Buddhist Thera is reversed as an elder who knows the tradition and may be advanced on his own path, but he clearly is not seen as having the same role in providing enlightenment to disciples as that of the Mahāyāna Zen master or the lama of Tibetan Vajrayāna. Similarly, living holy men in Eastern Orthodoxy have served as foci for disciples in a way comparable to Indic holy men, and Catholic monastic discipline retains the principle of obedience—but, as we shall see more closely toward the end of chapter 4, the role of the holy man as dominant focus in Protestant traditions can become problematic indeed.

These large-scale patterns of distribution of dominant foci in greater contexts can be understood, in part, through an examination of their distinctive characteristics identified in the introduction:

their concentrated or diffuse manifestation and their limited or limitless scope. Most easily combinable with other traditions, as we have now seen, are the "diffusely manifest" elements of a limited heritage. Within a diffuse heritage, a number of holy men may find places as distinct concentrations of the divine. And as long as they recognize the limitations of their scope they may remain compatible with one another. The singular personality, on the other hand, concentrated but with a limitless scope, is likely to develop into the most exclusive immanent focus. He stands, moreover, in particular tension with the holy man, both foci representing concentrated manifestations of spiritual power. For a singular-personality context to accommodate a holy man, the latter must be taken as an element in a "diffuse" heritage. The more diffuse the heritage becomes, the more vitally the role of the holy man can develop.

ii. Balance

While the most frequent context for the holy man is a developed heritage, the most fertile contexts are grounded in unifying truths that encompass all heritages. The holy man's revelation of a unifying truth's hidden secrets, depicted in figure 8, is certainly one dimension of the radical complementarity between the two foci. But this functional complementarity between the holy man and the unifying truth seems to reflect a deeper balance, a balance among the distinctive characteristics of the immanent foci that appears to underlie their recurrent combinations all over the world.

Though holy men declaring unifying truths that transcend any one world religion have sometimes flourished when high cultures come into contact, the world religions themselves have, for the last two millennia, generally presented viable combinations of eternal-heritage and singular-personality elements: devotional Hinduism; Catholic (including Eastern Orthodox) Christianity; Mahāyāna (and *popular* Theravāda) Buddhism. When we look at these two types of combinations—the holy man presenting a unifying truth and the ritual worship of deities prevalent in most world religions—we find that *each* contains *all* of the distinctive characteristics of the immanent foci. That is, each contains aspects of the limited and the limitless, the concentrated and the diffuse:

	concentrated	diffuse
limited	holy man	eternal heritage
limitless	singular personality	unifying truth

Figure 9.—The Dynamics of Balance among the Immanent Foci

It is suggestive for the state of contemporary religion that neither component of the "Judeo-Protestant" tradition often seen as formative for twentieth-century ways of life displays this sort of internal balance: Rabbinic Judaism admits no independent singular personality; Protestantism rejects a "Catholic" heritage. In chapter 4 we will suggest what the imbalance of these two traditions from our perspective might mean for the state of Western religion today. But first we will turn to the religious significance of the syntactic regularities themselves.

2. The Religio-Historical Implications of Grammatical Consistency

The balance found in the most common combinations of foci and the dynamic of hidden and revealed found in their transformations both point to a single principle of religious perception, one that will eventually help us understand better the force of the idea of sant tradition for devotees attempting to comprehend their gurus. The generality of this principle becomes clearer when the different oppositions on which our patterns of combination and transformation depend are reduced to more abstract contrasts, which show a basic similarity. To this end, we must analyze more closely the distinctive characteristics displayed by immanent foci, their possible dimensions as places at which people see the divine.

The manifestation of a focus, as we have seen, can be either concentrated or diffuse; its scope, limited or limitless. The first term of each of these oppositions refers to the way in which a focus appears *specific:* that is, definite, fixed—"concentrated," "limited." The second term refers to the way in which a focus appears *infinite:* that is, manifold, amorphous—"diffuse," "limitless." These two general categories, *specific* and *infinite,* also subsume the contrast between the revealed and hidden found to be crucial in the dynamic of transformation in tradition. For as long as a mystery is hidden it remains amorphous, susceptible to infinite interpretation; once it is revealed it becomes graspable in fixed, specific terms.

The immanent foci, then, work as symbols that bring the infinite and specific together in different ways. The complementary patterns presented by our syntax of foci, moreover, demonstrate the play between these two fundamental aspects of religious symbols in the socio-religious domain: a viable tradition necessarily projects the infinite qualities of the divine in some specific way that people can grasp. To this general principle all the large-scale patterns of religious tradition outlined above can be taken as corollaries.

a. The Infinite and Specific in Structures of Religio-Historical Syntax

First of all, we traced out two progressive transformations of tradition. One, of routinization, gives a specific holy man like Govind or Kabīr increasingly infinite dimensions. The other specifies the whole of an infinite heritage in one of its great personalities—who may then become immediately accessible through a very specific living teacher: Hinduism finds its essence in Krishna as presented by Vallabha. The dynamic of hidden and revealed through which these progressions evolve maintains a complementarity of infinite and specific between the salvational methods of traditions and their communal dimensions. Singular personalities—Buddha and Jesus—arise as salvational foci for infinitely diverse communities. Heritages develop when infinite saving grace is seen in specific communal traditions—those deriving from rooted cultural forms, as in Tibetan Buddhism, or those evolving in a complex sectarian organization, as in the Roman Catholic church. Holy men—lamas and abbots—may then emerge to reveal the specific ways of the infinite divine for both communal order and salvational means.

Traditions break down when either the infinite or the specific becomes seriously obscured. Corruption takes place when too much apparently unregenerate humanness makes links to the infinite divine seem visibly tenuous (recall the son of Ḍālādāsī in Ayodhyā and the scandalous *puṣṭimārgīya gosāīṃ*). When the revealed forms offered by a tradition no longer appear specifically relevant to contemporary adherents, that tradition collapses—normally into a diffuse heritage (the fate of some sant *panths*) or a limitlessly diffuse unifying truth (the fate of some Western religions today).

The combinations taken by the immanent foci among themselves demonstrate the restrictions that a dominant singular personality can impose on tradition. As a specifically concentrated focus with an infinite scope, the singular personality stands in tension with other concentrated foci of the divine. This tension is resolved only with the appearance of the diffuse dimension of the infinite in a heritage; the Tibetan lama stands as one of countless Buddhas in Tibetan Vajrayāna; the abbot's discipline is understood within an extended tradition of hierarchal authority. And since only the singular personality and eternal heritage combine both infinite and specific qualities, only these form the bases of lasting world religions.

The most widespread forms of the world religions, moreover—Roman Catholicism, Sunni Islam, and devotional Hinduism—are balanced by *both* heritage and personality elements, bringing together the infinite and specific in all their aspects. And personality-less Judaism and heritage-less Protestantism seem at least to present viable syntheses of the infinite and specific in the powerful dynamics of hidden and revealed that they characteristically maintain. In Judaism this dynamic works through holy men, who keep the tradition fertile in all its aspects: as Kabbalists they have never ceased finding new meanings in old texts; as rabbis they were in constant discussion over the law. Protestant tradition, as exemplified in Calvinism, offers a radical tension between a specific revealed scripture and an always unknown, very hidden elect—a classic dynamic of reform.

The holy man, concentrated and limited, presents specific dimensions without explicit infinite ones; and the universal truth, limitless and diffuse, is infinite but in no way specific. For this reason, neither of these two foci alone is likely to form a viable basis for tradition, and each, in fact, almost always appears in combination with other immanent foci. But since the holy man and a unifying truth are polar opposites, each also usually demands the presence of some complementary dimension of the other. Thus, a knowledgeable holy man within a particular variant of a world religion is likely to present a specific synthesis, unifying teachings from other variants of his own great tradition—together, perhaps, with some from outside it. And most of the coherent syntheses presented outside great religious contexts are identified as the teachings of specific, spiritually gifted individuals: e.g. the gnostic systems of Simon Magus, Valentinus, and Mani.

We observe, then, that within the world religions the holy man is usually taken as an element in a configuration of foci—a basis of faith very concentrated and very specific; a limitlessly diffuse unifying perspective, on the other hand, appears in an established tradition as a factor of greater religious context, open-ended, and amorphous. But when the holy man and a unifying truth come together outside the world religions the unifying truth may itself dominate the vision of serious seekers. Thus the wide-ranging theosophist exploring traditions where he can find them may be more committed to an open-ended quest than to any link to the divine to be derived from a single living teacher. While he may, to be sure, appreciate insights received from specific, spiritually gifted individuals along the way, none may command his allegiance for very long.

The quest of Kabīr, the first great Hindi sant, is sometimes said to have entailed a search on this order, open-ended and skeptical, moving, perhaps, from one guru to another.[15] But as sant tradition was becoming established, the followers of single living gurus had to make another sort of spiritual effort. These devotees had faith in definite holy men of concentrated focus and limited scope. They had somehow to add explicit infinite dimensions to the image of their gurus without denying the powerful specificity of the soteriological means their gurus offered. This dilemma of the sant's devotee lies at the heart of the problem of a holy-man theology. For a theological resolution of the dilemma would entail placing the guru in some sort of greater religious context. But just what would this context look like? A radical complementarity between the highly specific holy man and a diffusely infinite unifying truth does not appear ever to have provided a conception coherent enough to offer a stable basis for collective tradition. Lasting traditions usually consolidate around the more balanced concepts of personalities and heritages, and the routinized developments of sant tradition that we have seen are no exceptions. A more careful examination of the factors of religious perception giving rise to these developments among sants and their devotees may give us some insight into the limits of the holy man as a focus for tradition.

b. The Holy Man as Immanent Focus and Sant Tradition

How does the iconloclastic sant as a focus of tradition differ from holy men who clearly exist within the world religions? Certainly, the figures of Sufis, Hasids, and Zen Masters derive much of their meaning for the devotee from the greater religious contexts, respectively, of Islam, Judaism, and Buddhism. But in giving their particular meanings to the holy man, these greater religious contexts also do more: they augment his dimensions, giving him a particular place in the greater scheme of things. They set the holy man himself within a consistent world view of creation and salvation, and the specific tradition within which he stands in relation to other traditions past and present. But it does not require a great world religion to connect the idea of the holy man to a greater perspective of the world. The same purpose can be served by a small-scale tradition understood to be independent from a larger context but which nevertheless manages to provide a coherent theology. Thus, sant *panths* often evolve theologies that somehow link the living guru to a past sant taken as a singular personality and place the past sant himself in relation to the Hindu heritage.

The really perplexing problems of sant theology emerge not in the *panths* but among devotees of living sants, either solitary or in established lineages. To be sure, as long as the holy man really is being experienced as charismatic—from near or far—the devotee has few difficulties: with the guru's hidden divine nature revealed to him, he is able to perceive the infinite in a very accessible specific form. But this vision of the holy man is not one easily to be routinized; the difficulties begin when this spatial, experiential perception is, for whatever reason, no longer immediate, and the disciple must deal with a somewhat empty *idea* of the holy man in creation and salvation. The difficulties begin, that is, when the disciple must place the holy man as an abstract basis of faith into a greater religious context.

Many devotees of a holy man can probably be satisfied with a relatively unformed idea of a unified divine that somehow manifests in different ways through individual holy men, especially since many holy men—like Śākyamuni during his lifetime and several Radhasoami masters[16]—normally tell people not to worry too much about metaphysical questions but to "follow the path." In this way, individual devotees can bring together specific impressions of their guru and private apprehensions of an infinite unity to find greater contexts for their faith. But the holy man and the unifying truth do not thus come together as an integrated theological basis for tradition.

Now a relatively unformed notion of the holy man reflecting unity can be particularly understandable to people with backgrounds in Hinduism, where the divine can manifest itself in lakes and images, and living people, too. Such Hindu sentiment could easily get bruised, however, when sants sang about the guru in glowing terms, but referred to sacred waters and images in language of abuse. Indeed, Pandit Faqir Chand, one of the more unorthodox gurus in the Radhasoami lineage, admits to having had a hard time with his guru's attitude on this score.[17] And while we can only speculate about how close the internal experience of different sants was, it is clear that the forms of traditional religions evoked in many the same *aversions*.

Thus, while most sants certainly did speak of a unifying truth—the one who was both Rām and Rahīm in medieval India—they usually did so in reductive rather than integral ways: that is, their characteristic assertion is that there is a truth beyond all the empty forms of religion, not that the one truth manifests on many legitimate paths. Since several of the sants further disclaimed being Hindu in any specifically religious sense, and a number of important ones were nominally Muslim, a liberal perception of holy men derived from the integrally unifying Hindu heritage would not suffice for many of their devotees. We thus arrive at the perception of a more specific heritage of sants: a diffuse but limited group of holy men who really know an eternal (but specific) truth beyond traditional religious forms.

Yet even this sant heritage, taken in a general sense, is not specific enough for many people revering definite lineages, where definite inner experiences appear to be transmitted through the spiritual generations. Contemporary Radhasoamis can further face an especially acute tension in having a clearly codified set of specific spiritual practices—which to their credit seems to be vital and effective—within a universe extending far beyond India. Thus, Radhasoamis who do not elevate Soamiji to a specific singular personality are at least likely to cherish ideas about masters throughout the world religions who have long maintained the heritage of doctrine and practice that is now available through Radhasoami initiation.

Standing outside any greater religious context, the sant as holy man is too specific a focus to provide a rationale for the routinized practice of an extended community. Yet merely seeing the sant in the context of an integrally amorphous unifying truth suggests spiritual possibilities too infinite to confirm the faith of a community of devotees engaged in specific practice. Thus, as a context for their individual gurus, a limited yet still open-ended sant tradition with a defined role in the economy of salvation could become a viable concept for devotees of later sants. In its Indian cultural environment this sant tradition appears as an extended clan with parallels in political and social worlds; in terms of our metacultural framework it appears as a heritage. Still, however it is described and whatever form it takes, the understanding of the sants as a tradition does seem to have existed—and indeed to have been called for by some fundamental principles of religious perception.

NOTES

/1/ For a description of this worship, see my *Lord as Guru*, p. 98.
/2/ A. P. Mathur, a guru at Agra tells us that the Radhasoami movement is "a new religion based on sant traditions": Agam Prasad Mathur, *Radhasoami Faith* (Delhi: Vikas, 1974), p. 75.
/3/ Lekh Raj Puri, writing from a Beas perspective, proclaims that "*Radha Swami Mat is Sant Mat pure and simple*" (his emphasis): *Radha Swami Teachings*, 2nd. ed. (Beas, Punjab: Radhasoami Satsang, 1972), p. 17.
/4/ Some of the intricacies of Radhasoami theology are presented in my *Lord as Guru*, ch. 6.
/5/ See my "Clan and Lineage among the Sants" in *The Sants: Studies in a Devotional Tradition of India*, ed. Karine Schomer and W. H. McLeod, Berkeley Religious Studies Series (Berkeley: Graduate Theological Union and Delhi: Motilal Banarsi Dass, 1987).
/6/ Classic works on religious symbol by these authors include: Mircea Eliade, *Patterns in Comparative Religion* (New York: Meridien, 1963); Paul Ricoeur, *The Symbolism of Evil* (Boston: Beacon Press, 1969), Victor Turner, *The Forest of Symbols: Aspects of Ndembu Ritual* (Ithaca and London: Cornell University Press, 1967).
/7/ The problem of the paucity of Ramaite sectarian traditions is suggested by John Stratton Hawley, *Sūr Dās* (Seattle: University of Washington Press, 1984), pp. 123–124.
/8/ See Mathur, *Radhasoami Faith*, p. 127.
/9/ The court cases stemmed from a charge of libel made by a *gosāīṃ* in 1861 against a *puṣṭimārgīya* reformer, Karsondās Muljī. In his defense, Muljī brought forward persons who gave eyewitness accounts of the adulterous behavior of the *gosāīṃs*, and he won the case. A transcript of the scandalous "Maharaj Libel Case" has been published and reprinted (Bombay: D. Lukhmidass and Co., 1911); four years after the trial Muljī published an inflammatory *History of the Sect of the Maharajas*. (London: Trubner and Co, 1865).
/10/ See Wendy Doniger O'Flaherty *The Problem of Evil in Indian Mythology* (Berkeley and Los Angeles: University of California Press, 1976), pp. 286–91.
/11/ Ram Dass, *Miracle of Love: Stories about Neem Karoli Baba* (New York: Dutton, 1979), pp. 289–99, describes the practical teachings on sex of a well-known, non-Westernized guru and gives accounts of subtle sexual interaction with women disciples.

/12/ See Geoffrey Moorehouse, *The Missionaries* (Philadelphia: Lippincott, 1973), pp. 324–25, 339–42.
/13/ See Khaliq Ahmad Nizami, *Some Aspects of Religion and Politics in India During the Thirteenth Century* (Delhi: Idarah-i Adabiyat-i Delli, 1974), pp. 175–76.
/14/ The relationships between Sufis and Shi'is are discussed by J. Spencer Trimingham, *The Sufi Orders in Islam* (New York: Oxford University Press, 1971), pp. 133–137.
/15/ The possibility of multiple gurus for Kabīr has been suggested by Pārаśurām Cāturvedī, the foremost Hindi scholar on the sants *(Uttarī Bhārat kī Sant Paramparā,* 3rd ed. [Allahabad: Leader Press, 1972]; it has been found plausible by Charlotte Vaudeville, Kabīr's most important Western interpreter *(Kabīr* [Oxford: Oxford University Press, 1974], p. 116). Still, it is likely that there was some one guru with whom Kabīr had a particularly close relationship; the different arguments about Kabīr's guru are treated in my *Lord as Guru,* pp. 107–109.
/16/ The three famous metaphysical questions that lead not to edification are found in the Aggi Vacchagotta Sutta *(Majjhima Nikāya* 1:484–488, translated by I. B. Horner, *The Collection of Middle Length Sayings* [London: Luzac and Co., 1957], pp. 162–167). For a Radhasoami master on bookish knowledge, see Kirpal Singh *Heart to Heart Talks,* vol. 1 (Delhi: Ruhani Satsang, 1972), p. 19.
/17/ Faqir Chand Ji Maharaj, *The Art of Happy Living,* trans. Prof. B. R. Kamal (Hoshiarpur, Punjab: Faqir Library Charitable Trust), pp. 26–27.

CHAPTER 4

THE POWERS OF THE GRAMMAR

Capable of being used to investigate problems beyond themselves, the immanent foci—like the sprayable electrons that impressed Ian Hacking[1]—seem to have a reality of their own. They appear grounded in human perceptions of the infinite and specific, becoming manifest in the broad patterns through which the world religions have evolved. Understood in this way, they help provide some answers to our questions about the emergence of the idea of sant tradition. At the same time, the categories designed to solve our immediate problems are also offered to a general community of scholars as a set of nodes around which some collective religio-historical knowledge might converge. And if others should use them to help solve *their* problems, not only might the immanent foci be used for comparing widely divergent materials, they are also liable to come together in different ways for grammatical analysis.

1. Some Linguistic Analogies

When taken from diverse religio-historical perspectives, the immanent foci are not likely always to seem as firmly grounded in religious perception as they may to us now. Scholars using the foci in their own ways will also probably have their own understandings of their reality. In general, the deeper the grounds in religious perception attributed to the immanent foci, the greater their potential explanatory power. We can distingiush three degrees of power at which the grammatical framework constituted by the immanent foci is able to work, each demanding a greater theoretical investment, and each with its own linguistic analogies.

At its weakest power, the grammar offers a flexible mode of approach toward continuous fields of religious phenomena, complex landscapes that need to be mapped out. In this mode, the grammar's only theoretical demand is an assent to the reasonableness of its categories: if viable patterns among the exuberant growths of Indian religion can be discerned through an analysis of foci in contexts, perhaps the same approach can be taken to other religio-cultural areas as well. Thus, the intricate religious worlds of China and the Ancient Near East show deities and rituals in a variety of overlapping traditions. What would happen if we employed our grammar in one of those areas?

In China, for example, we might speak of the interaction of the Confucian and Taoist heritages and their assimilation of the Buddhist tradition that looks to a personality from the West. Buddha, Confucius, and Lao-tze, then—together with the Bodhisattvas, celestial bureaucrats, and divine animals of popular Chinese lore—become personalities within converging heritages. Though starting with the immanent foci as general categories, we will probably be led to particular, context-bound distinctions among them. What, for example, might the importance in traditional China of both the worshipful veneration of the dead and a physically conceived immortality mean for the broad contrast we have made between the often-dead singular personality and the necessarily embodied holy man? As we delve deeper into our particular problems, moreover, we may want to abandon our technical vocabulary completely, concentrating instead on the differences, say, between the dead and venerated sage of the past and the embodied Taoist immortal. At its lowest power, then, the grammar presents us with a framework of foci in contexts as an initial avenue for understanding complex fields—a framework that may let specific categories evolve according to particular materials and problems.

Used in this way, as an approach to mapmaking, the grammatical framework has a value that is almost entirely pragmatic—effective for the scholar but not necessarily real for the religious subject. This general attitude toward the value of analytic concepts was current in the positivist American linguistics of the Bloomfieldian era. So not surprisingly, the relevant linguistic analogies presented by the grammar at its lowest power are with the -emic and morphological approaches for which the Bloomfieldians are distinguished.[2] How can we parse a connected field of religious phenomena into significantly distinct forms? What changes do these forms undergo when they appear in particular combinations and distinct contexts?

The grammar takes on a higher degree of power when it is

used to analyze phenomena in *discontinuous* religio-historical fields. From a means of understanding complex patterns of religion *within* India or China, the grammar now becomes a basis for systematic comparisons *between* two such disparate regions. Are there any ways in which the relationship between past sages and embodied immortals in China parallel the continuities we have seen between past teachers and living holy men in India? Can we draw larger religio-cultural contrasts from the different ways in which human and divine beings are distinguished in the two areas? When taken at this intermediate power, the grammar in fact "intermediates" between traditions.

Used in this way, the grammar demands a greater theoretical investment than when it is used as a starting place for the development of a set of distinctions appropriate for a single continuous field. For if taken seriously as stable points of reference for concepts appearing in diverse cultures, its fundamental categories must be understood to reflect some essential human commonalities. No longer merely useful, the immanent foci must now represent distinctions that are psychologically real.

At this intermediate power, the immanent foci become analogous to the general categories of syntax used by linguists of universal (and not so universal) vision: the "nominals" and "verbals" familiar in traditional and modern grammar; the "case relations" taken by some linguists as basic. These general syntactic categories certainly make implicit affirmations about the way reality is normally perceived, even though the general affirmations that they posit can have obviously different structural entailments in different cultural worlds. As the most familiar categories of the linguist presuppose that most everyday perception is ultimately that "something (nominal) happens (verbal)," so the immanent foci, in this intermediate power, presuppose that religious perception normally finds a base in faith—which is usually directed toward people, gods, and traditions.

The grammar takes on its strongest power when the immanent foci are understood not only to be viable comparative categories, but also to present consistent relationships across cultures. These relationships then seem to indicate some universal principles of religious perception, which call for explanation. How are we to understand any possible universal dimensions to the patterns that emerge from comparative analysis? Linguists discussing universals sometimes distinguish two kinds of universals: strong, and weak.[3] Strong universals, envisioned by Chomsky and his school, attempt to identify specific linguistic capacities that would be reflected in a systematic universal grammar of a definite shape. Weak universals, formulated by participants in Greenberg's project at Stanford, provide explanations for recurrent grammatical patterns in terms of general psychological factors. Forming no complex grammar and explained in terms of general factors of perception, the universals offered in this book appear more like Greenberg's weak ones.[4]

Indeed, the closest analogy to our approach toward universals here might be found in a particular development of the Greenbergian program that explains the recurrence together of basic syntactic patterns through reference to a simple underlying rule of linguistic behavior. The categories that combine to form the patterns are reduced to more fundamental ones, and the patterns recurring together are shown to reveal a consistent order at the more fundamental level. Human beings, then, may be understood to order the same types of categories consistently in a single language.[5] Here, too, the characteristic of the basic categories (limited/limitless; concentrated; revealed/hidden) are reduced to one fundamental contrast (specific/infinite), but the principles arrived at emerge not from simple syntactic ordering, but from the interaction of a syntax of configurations of foci with a semantics of religious meanings: how do the significances of formally combinable elements regulate their normal occurrence together?

With its closed set of categories capable of endless combination, its basis in principles of perception, and its linguistic analogies, the grammar at its most powerful can be seen to offer an explanation of the type often thought of as structuralist.[6] But the broad-scale structuralist claims made here are less radical than those found in the classical structuralist program of Claude Levi-Strauss, whose binary oppositions have been frequently interpreted as a sweeping transference of simple phonemic contrasts to all of human thought.[7] The binary contrasts of this analysis are limited to factors of specifically religious perception. Our argument offers a more restricted approach, recalling that of linguists who attempt to move from broad-scale regularities of language patterning to particular statements about language and mind.[8] Here we move from consistent patterns of development in religious tradition to some universal statements about a particular vital dimension of religious perception, one that recognizes the structure of foundations, an object of faith's particular *form*.

Taken in their lowest power as well as their highest, the

categories of our grammar, like those in most fields of knowledge, begin to be perceived as real only when they are used. They must be helpful for pragmatists, provide insight for comparativists, and fit neatly into the schemes of systematic thinkers. When, through use, a set of concepts achieves about as much reality as it is going to have for any of these types of thinkers, perhaps it can offer a basis for some serious discourse among them. There will be criticisms and qualifications, to be sure. Nevertheless, systematists may have to take account of the results of pragmatists' meanderings over their own particular religio-cultural areas; and pragmatists may in turn be guided in *their* explorations through systematists' patterns. If scholars at these two extremes do take account of one another, they are likely to be drawn toward the middle—universal systems becoming less precise, and cultural specifics leading to more general speculation. It is in this realm of limited generalizations and particular, multi-focused comparisons where religio-historical knowledge is most likely to accumulate.

Certainly, the primary practical import of the immanent foci is for knowledge in this middle range, toward which the intermediate power of the grammar makes the largest contribution. The foci are clearly not *necessary* for exploring continuous fields, where categories may emerge directly from specific materials. And their systematic implications may well have already been exhausted in the preceding chapter of this book. Yet in order to formulate believable, middle-range statements about general religious phenomena we must use concepts that are at least theoretically independent of any one tradition. For with no comparative framework that can intermediate among disparate religious worlds, how can we identify *either* what is common to religious life *or* what distinguishes one tradition from another?

2. The Indian Guru and Western Traditions: A Grammatical Interpretation

An extended example may help illustrate the potential of the immanent foci as categories of intermediate range, terms that can help us juxtapose the dynamics of different religious situations. We will still deal with problems of India, holy men, and sants, but in a way perhaps more relevant than elsewhere in this book to many Western readers—of whom the majority may know Indian gurus primarily by their numbers who have come to the West. Do these gurus play the same roles here as they do in India? Are their devotees' attitudes similar? And if the West has its own traditions of holy men, what are we doing with Indian gurus here at all? What, finally, is the particular place of the sants among Indian gurus in the West today? By letting us move back and forth among a number of traditions in the East and West, the immanent foci will help us answer these questions. Starting from the West we begin with Judaism, for structural as well as historical reasons. Not only is Judaism the oldest of the Western traditions to be treated, but as an eternal heritage it also offers a nice comparison with Hinduism in India.

a. The Holy Man in Western Traditions: Classical Patterns

At the beginning of the Christian era Israel knew messianic zealots, mystically inclined sectarian traditions, as well as many scholars well versed in religious law. The rabbinic Judaism that grew up after the destruction of the second temple developed the scholarly strain, and the heritage that emerged articulated itself in an idiom of *knowledge*. But this was a very different type of knowledge from the Buddhist insight into essential realities or even the Hindu knowledge of the formless brahman. It was, rather, a discursive thought (often more intuitive and analogic than strictly reasoned) grounded in a thorough familiarity with traditional texts. The intellectual paradigm is the *legal debate*.

Now in brahminic India, which like the rabbinic world knew a complex ritual heritage, there was just as much customary law, but there the customs seem to have been taken more for granted, and intellectual speculation ranged freely to metaphysics. There were certainly "legal" *dharma śāstras* (which dealt in large part with problems of inheritance); but local customs were fixed enough and generally perceived to be "eternal" enough that active pondering on how to adapt traditional law to specific situations did not develop into the central manifestation of intellectual culture that it did in Judaism.[9] More fundamental to the intellectual culture was *mīmāṃsā*, which treats problems of interpretation necessary to perform a correct *sacrifice*. In Judaism, however, applying Torah to concrete and occasionally very hypothetical situations remained the dominant intellectual strand, and involved lengthy discourses about "things" and their relationships in the world. The Kabbalistic mysticism that developed within rabbinic Judaism internalized just this kind of intellectual culture—as exemplified in the early speculation on the complex interrelationships of ten "spheres" and their manifold attributes in the "four worlds." A famous aphorism asserts that one was supposed to have studied Talmud till he was forty before taking up Kabbalah. At any rate, Kabbalistic mysticism was firmly grounded in the lettered rabbinic tradition and was literally "unthinkable" without it.

The paradigmatic relationship of the disciple to his master in the mystical varieties of Judaism, then, was that of the student to a teacher who had mastered the traditional knowledge. Such mastery necessarily implied high spiritual qualifications, and could be seen as theurgically effective enough to give the rabbi an exalted position. But even when the rabbi was seen as a highly qualified master of powerful spiritual knowledge, both his image for his disciples and his relation to tradition differed decidedly from those of the Hindu guru. The latter was seen to be a *deva*, a "divine being" dispensing flowing grace, with whom the devotee could ultimately merge his identity in a world perceived as a continuity of matter. As a *deva* the yogic guru could stand independent of his lettered heritage in a way not normative in Judaism: Hindu lore frequently presents an opposition between the brahmin, well versed in traditional matters but usually not very charismatic, and the accomplished ascetic, powerful but often inarticulate and with little use for books. A tension of the same type does not appear in Jewish tradition until the rise of Hasidism, presaging the modern period. It is worth noting, however, that even here the famous complaint of the illustrious Vilna *gaon* against the Hasids was not that they were mystics—the *gaon* himself was an eminent Kabbalist—but that they were attempting to be mystics without *also* being scholars.[10]

The rabbinic heritage, in addition to providing moderate accommodation for the holy man, also had room for a few featured personalities, the most important no doubt being "Moses Our Rabbi" and the Messiah to come. But the significance of these is dominated by their relation to aspects of the heritage itself; from a comparative perspective their own personal figures remain fairly undeveloped—Moses Our Rabbi "gave us the law"; the Messiah is a figure ushering in Israel's political and eschatological glory.[11]

In forms of Christian tradition, however, figures of singular personalities become well elaborated indeed. Jesus, whatever his sectarian background, did present a variant of the religion of Israel more devotional and more immediately amenable to popular mysticism than that which grew up among the rabbis. Among the gentiles this devotional variant evolved in an (Indo-Aryan?) way that featured developed personalities more comparable with the Hindu divinities. The legend and iconography surrounding the figures of Jesus and Mary are certainly as elaborate as anything found in Hindu tradition; and analogies can clearly be seen between the existence of distinct local Madonnas, all representing the Mother of Our Lord, and the identification of local Indian *devīs* with the great goddess.

As with divine beings among the Hindus, Jesus and Mary in their different aspects—together with a vast assembly of saints—could be dealt with personally by devotees and called upon for grace. But the Christian devotee did not normally become *absorbed* in his immediate object of devotion as a Hindu might. The Indian divinities, further, could stand as independent sources of grace within the great Hindu heritage; but the saints of the Roman Catholic Church all necessarily found a link to Jesus as a singular personality through a network rooted in a definite line of apostolic succession. With this network of channels of grace—no doubt the most firmly structured on such a scale that the history of religions has ever seen—the abbot of a monastery could assume the role of holy man for monks in his charge, who were bound to vows of obedience. Even if he himself was of only moderate spiritual attainment, he could certainly fulfill some practical psychological roles in the religious development of those under his discipline, humbling the devotee when necessary and provding a trusted ideal. In Eastern Orthodox Christianity, with its less tightly organized structures, the reclusive ascetic could also serve functions for the public at large more directly comparable to the popular Indian holy man.[12]

Western Protestant Christianity, in rejecting not only the Papacy but also much previous tradition, gave the individual even more spiritual independence. But its characteristic style of piety was not at all consonant with the role of the holy man as focus found in Catholic Christianity as well as in India. In Hindu tradition the disciple is bound closely to his guru in a highly personal way; but once he understands what it means to make an ultimate identification with his master, he can become, like the master, absolutely spiritually independent. In the Roman Church, the master as (a rather attenuated) focus is a link in a chain; he may impose discipline on those in his charge, but their identities remain separate, and he himself may be subject to higher ecclesiastical authority. Protestant tradition breaks the chain, and the individual looks only to the Lord and His Divine Personality, with no possibility of intervention by any other being. The individual is bound to no one but the Lord, but he can never become absolutely independent like Him.

The Catholic and Protestant approaches to spiritual independence looked to different precedents and implied different values. Thus a liberal Roman Catholic thinker like Erasmus respected the consensus of the tradition he knew and, valuing the unity of Christendom, attempted to keep his position adequately consonant with that of the majority. The Protestant reformers contemporary with him, on the other hand, recognized authority in faith and scripture, recalling the just remnant of Israel and the virtue of the righteous minority.[13] In practice this led to the emergence of a number of different sectarian movements (each with its own righteous, minority opinion) developing in diverse socio-religious directions: communal, charismatic, and evangelistic.

When they evangelized among non-European peoples, Protestant missionaries, unused to ritual, were often less flexible than the Catholic ones in dealing religiously with the various cultural heritages they encountered. A few Protestant missionaries in India, however, early took interest in Kabīr and the Kabīr *panth*, seeing in the famous sant a "reformer" after the model of their own spiritual heroes.[14] And some of the comparisons certainly do stand. Both the early sants and the early Protestant reformers stressed an internalization of religion at the expense of ritual form. And Kabīr, as well as a number of other sants, adopted a missionizing attitude more popular and radically outspoken than is usual in post-classical Hindu tradition—and which may be partly accounted for by an input from Western religion via the social role in India of a particular type of Sufi.

But this missionizing attitude of the sant as holy man was often tempered by the image of the Hindu yogi as guru—which is different indeed from that of the missionizing Christian evangelical. The former is traditionally supposed to have himself reached attainment under the guidance of a guru, and is fulfilling his *dharma* by offering spiritual shelter to those who come to him. He deals with his disciples individually as far as possible and can appear to them as a stable spiritual source, a trustworthy basis of faith. The evangelical has ideally experienced a calling from the Lord to propagate His word throughout man's world. He thus often seeks fulfillment in an attempt to lead large numbers of people to find the kingdom of heaven—and if successful can appear to them in the guise of a Messiah.

The role of the yogi can certainly be abused by someone of mistaken or unbalanced attainments (or by just a plain fraud), who may inflict a limited amount of psychic or material harm on individuals; but as we have seen in the still remembered Jonestown tragedy, an "independent" Protestant leader taken in a messianic guise—who then distorts his role by enforcing *discipline* on an isolated community—can do massive collective damage by almost anyone's standards. Obedience to a figure standing within the channels of grace from Rome, however, will not lead as easily to the same type of consequences. For with all that can be said against the high-handed means by which the Roman Church has at times suppressed heresy, the weighty apostolic heritage it supports does have the effect of checking the operative authority of the *idiosyncratically* psychopathic.

b. The Indian Guru and Religion in the West Today

The contemporary age has seen the rise of a secular culture that dominates the life and thought of most Westerners. This secular culture—which finds intellectual roots in Enlightenment rationalism and uses an idiom of empiric science—coexists (not always very happily) with established Western religious currents. Especially in America, where the secular culture has reached its materialistic apogee, these currents have been identified as characteristically Judaeo-Protestant, with reference to the Calvinistic invocation of legal and radically monotheistic values found especially in the Hebrew scriptures. The grammatical treatment of socio-religious problems will give a somewhat novel turn to otherwise well-explored approaches to the relationships among Judaism, Protesantism, and modern Western "rationality," one which may lead to a new perspective on the place of the Indian guru in the modern West.

i. Imbalance, Disintegration, and the Rise of the Secular Culture

Our study of the recurrent combinations of the immanent foci has shown us a particular type of *imbalance* within rabbinic Judaism and Protestant Christianity: while most forms of the world religions present effective practical amalgamations of personality and heritage elements, neither of these traditions does. Compared with most other forms of the world religions, Protestantism lacks a developed heritage of myth and ritual, while Judaism lacks significant devotional personalities. The development of both these traditions in such extreme directions may be partially explained in terms of *reaction*. Initial Protestant rejection of much of the accumulated Christian heritage comes as a response to the perceived corruption of Catholic institutions. And the reluctance of European Jews to develop fully the personality resources in fact contained in rabbinic tradition may derive from their diaspora existence within a surrounding religious culture that has usurped (and in Jewish eyes perverted) some of the most vital of these resources.

But whatever the decisive factors in their development as such, traditions "unbalanced" in our sense usually present highly differentiated—often very rigorous—norms, but no intermediate foci to provide alternative religious options. These traditions seem to work well for homogeneous groups composed in good part of individuals with lesser or greater spiritual gifts—as Weber would call them, the "religiously musical" and "virtuosos."[15] But they face problems adapting to changed conditions and serving constituencies of the religiously less musical unable to adhere to pristine norms.

Traditions "unbalanced" toward the singular personality side are oriented toward spare goals that impose severe restrictions on the few. For the many, of course, these goals are practically (though sometimes only implicitly) modified, but the force of the restrictions that they ideally demand retains an effect on the development of the less rigorous forms of tradition. This pattern of development is evident in both Calvinistic Protestantism and Pālī Buddhism, traditions that we have identified as having extreme singular-personality orientations and that Weber presented as radical examples of his types.[16] The Weberian types represented, however, are diametrically opposed: the inner-worldly ascetic *versus* the other-worldly mystic.

The Pālī canonical tradition—which Weber took as "Buddhism"—does in fact seem sooner to reflect the concerns of other-worldly monks than of common laymen. It offers monks a moderately ascetic meditative ideal, but one which could be emulated in a less rigorous form by lay followers—who were also to support the *sangha*, the monastic order. But in developed Theravāda societies, the contrast between lay and monastic ideals becomes more sharply defined. Since a pure and thriving *sangha* is seen as a prerequisite for society's prosperity, for many householders the surest path toward success in this world and the next appears as support for the *sangha* through offerings of food and sons—acts that not only maintain the world order but also accord personal merit. Indeed, many laymen understand the most practicable path to salvation as one of accumulating enough merit to be born during the lifetime of Maitreya, the coming Buddha, who will effect their release without the necessity for strenuous meditation on their own part. Living up to an ideal of meditation practice grounded in spiritual knowledge is difficult for common monks too, and some of the most enthusiastic meditators today seem to be not monks at all, but newly inspired lay *upāsakas*. Most monks tend to emphasize their role as teachers, not meditators, and the mark of their purity in the *dhamma* is their visible adherence to the traditional rule of discipline.[17]

The codified monastic formulations of Theravāda, which provide the monk with his minimum standard of purity, seem to affect restrictions on many other aspects of the tradition. For the monks who do meditate, these restrictions lead both to a fairly homogeneous development of practice that looks to the canon and a few classic texts, and the lack of well differentiated lineages of teachers and deities of the types frequent in Vajrayāna. The laity have a full-bodied mythology to be sure (featuring in large part the many lives of the Buddha as singular personality), but no developed hagiographical tradition lauding holy men, and a ritual life that remains, by Indic (and East Asian) standards, relatively spare.

Protestantism, for Weber, found its most radically characteristic formulation in Calvinist doctrine. In this formulation God has created man in the world for His own glory but remains Himself transcendent, absolutely separate from both man and the world; man serves God's glory by striving to attain His kingdom on earth according to the revealed law. The Calvinist expression of these understandings, as Weber has shown, is congruent, at least, with significant aspects of the temper that success in a capitalistic, increasingly bureaucratic society demands. But as Weber also knew, once such a society is set up, people can function in it very well without actively adhering to Calvinistic tenets. Many eventually did, and even within Calvinism doctrines began to develop in less severe directions. But important restrictive norms implied by the radical tenets have had a lasting effect on the more moderate Protestant culture. The specification of righteous action in the world as the way to serve God's glory has not encouraged the sort of devotion to inner life sometimes found in monasteries, and so has led to the development of no *cultivated* mystical paths. Nor has the absolute separation between the fleshly and the divine supported the development of much ritual life.

A Lord who was not to be experienced internally through regular means and who left no signs in a heritage of myth and ritual could slip from the grasp of many brought up in Protestant traditions. For such persons Jehovah could indeed become "otiose," as in the non-literate cultures Mircea Eliade has written about[18]—but in this instance there was no specifically religious image to replace Him. Many modern Jews find themselves in a similar religious situation, though they have arrived there by a different route.

A tradition like Judaism, with an extreme eternal-heritage orientation presents even the religiously unmusical individuals with a way of life in which the "sacred"—whatever its value for them—cannot be ignored. But the way of life that such a tradition presents is a self-contained one, which can undergo severe difficulties when disrupted. One of the closest parallels to an extreme rabbinic heritage to be found in the history of religions is the piety of traditional brahmins. For Jews and brahmins both, ritual practice was the prerogative of a specific hereditary group and served to mark it as distinct. But in India the brahmins found a place for themselves within a complex hierarchy of castes, and served important ritual functions for the society as a whole.

For the Jews, however, there was a single primary distinction between Israel and the gentiles, who had their own religious specialists. To the gentiles, of course, it was the Jews who were the outcastes, but unto themselves the Jews were the brahmins—"a nation of priests." And as such they managed in the diaspora to develop a pattern of living that brought together specialized economic functions *vis-à-vis* the gentiles, more diverse socio-economic interaction among themselves, and a full ritual life within their own communities. With the emancipation of the Western Jews in the nineteenth century these communities began to fall apart, and Jews living in the secular world were forced to find new ways to be religious. Comparable problems were faced by modern brahmins, though as we shall shortly see, there were ways they could be religious through devotional foci in the Hindu heritage without being rigorously brahminic. Modern Jews, however, could not follow a similar course and still retain a Jewish identity (*pace* modern Hebrew Christians). And for many modern Jews, Jehovah, with no accessible focus in the world, began to appear otiose indeed.

Jews and Protestants who had lost touch with vital religious foci were often very enthusiastic in their embrace of the truths of the Enlightenment. The wholehearted acceptance of a worldly rationality by many Jews and Protestants would make sense in terms of Weber's systematic comparison of religions: he saw both Judaism and Protestantism as "inner-worldly" (as opposed to "other-worldly") and both as characteristically *rational*. Weber devoted much attention to the topic of rationality, which he took very generally to mean the organization of experience in some systematic way, but which he saw as having a number of different varieties.[19]

While Protestant tradition may show a lack of developed mystical paths and ritual, it certainly does not lack a rational rigor. As an attempt to make intellectual sense out of a religious insight, a radical doctrine of predestination is certainly a severely *consistent* entailment of a vision of man's helplessness in the face of an almighty power. Weber saw the characteristic Calvinist expression of such Protestant rationality in purposeful, calculated action toward an outward goal, a type of rationality he also saw as the distinctive component of a modern, increasingly bureaucratic society. But a Calvinist religious perspective was also most consonant with the rationality of a scientist: for though God was separate from the world, the world contained His law, which was likely to be constant since predestined, and thus ascertainable through outwardly directed empiric research.

Among the rabbis Weber identified a more traditional type of rationality, no doubt connected with the approach we have seen the rabbis taking to religious truth through concrete, discursive thought, often of a very well-reasoned nature. As the Jews began to take part in the new secular order, their traditional type of rationality was successfully adapted to professional endeavor and capitalistic enterprise. But it was the mystical turn a rabbinic way of thinking could take—a turn unfamiliar to Protestant rationality—that was to have the most profound consequences for the enlightened secular culture.

The Kabbalistic mystic, as we have observed, let the apparently "rational" manipulation of symbols loaded at once with psychic, cosmic, and historical meanings carry his religious sensibilities along in a connected and wide-ranging discourse, a discourse that indeed comprehended the limits of his perception. Toward the close of the nineteenth century, as scientific man was beginning to evolve comprehensive world-views on materialistic presuppositions, such concrete but multidimensional thinking turned out to be appropriate for supplying the requisite depth to upset old convictions and establish new ones. Men who in another age would have been Kabbalists taking their weighty symbolic discourse to the depths of the soul, the limits of space, and the triumphant role of the righteous community were able to do so just as well within various material frames of reference. So while Protestants were presenting the secular culture with a doctrine of empiric method, the Jews were providing it with *mysteries:* psychoanalysis, relativity, dialectic materialism.

ii. Liberal Traditions, Gurus, and Sants

The twentieth-century secular culture and *its* mysteries have submitted the established forms of Western religion to considerable stress. The difficulties to which this stress has led can be readily understood in terms of the problems of *adaptation* and *making distinctions* identified in chapter 1 as crucial to the immanent foci manifesting respectively in time and space. The problems of adaptation in time are most basic: how do adherents of a tradition relate its inspired teachings to the truths of science and its forms of practice to the conditions of industrial society? But twentieth-century communications, in making visible a highly variegated world culture, have also created special problems of making distinctions in space—problems recalling those of the early sants. Emerging during an extended period of confrontation between Hinduism and Islam, the sants and were led to revalue traditional religio-cultural distinctions in face of an obvious religious plurality.[20] Today, similar problems of religious plurality occur in a considerably different form and on a much vaster scale: how do members of a tradition perceive its uniqueness in a world in which the visible coexistence of many religions is inescapable?

To these problems Western religion has offered both conservative responses, subordinating the modern patterns to long-established traditions, and liberal ones, radically reinterpreting past ways of thought and practice. But Jews and Christians find different types of problems particularly troublesome. With long experience as a minority within a varied diaspora, the Jews were well versed in religious plurality; and in a heritage context of obviously limited scope, some notion of the legitimacy of other traditions in their proper place is likely to be taken for granted. For the Jews the pressing problem was to adapt their traditional practices into some viable form of modern religion. Since the industrial life-style developed within a Christian culture, Christians had fewer difficulties in adapting forms of traditional religious practice; but—looking to a magnificent singular personality—they could have serious problems with religious plurality. Thus a conservative response for the Jew ("orthodox" in native categories) shows up in elaborate forms of ritual practice; for the Christian, in doctrinal rigidity.

Now the religion of elaborate everyday ritual faces serious problems *anywhere* the modern technicalistic culture has had a serious impact, and the brahmin attempting to do bustling business in Bombay can face just the same kind of adjustments in trying to be orthodox as the observant Jew working in New York. For the urban brahmin, however, there are ways of actively participating in religion that are less ritually demanding. Hindus of any caste can turn to forms of worship featuring singular personalities or to holy men who have passed beyond the realm of rites—both of which have burgeoned in the Indian cities.[21] Both, of course, have ancient precedent, and can also appear together with various degrees of "conservative" ritual. Jews, however, have no such options open to them, and for them to be religious in any traditional sense entails a fair amount of demanding ritual observance.

Christians, like Hindu *bhaktas*, look to a singular personality, but even more than sectarian Hindus, conservative Christians assert His uniqueness and the absolute truth of a particular (usually fairly literal) reading of His word. The liberals are ecumenicals, seeking to minimize distinctions first among Christian traditions and then among the religions of the world. Both Catholic and Protestant Christianity show a wide spectrum of conservative and liberal forms, though the Catholic apostolic heritage makes for restraint in both directions. It is among the Protestants, then, that we find both the conservative *and* the liberal extremes.

Protestant and Jewish traditions at the liberal extremes serve individuals whose conscious presuppositions about the universe are framed, for the most part, in the scientific idiom of secular culture. They present aspects of traditional Western mysteries in terms that these individuals can somehow comprehend. The force of potent myth and consistent cosmology does not generally come across in the translation, however, and a coherent synthesis of Western theological concepts and the truths of science has yet to evolve. The liberal traditions do provide vehicles for those who want to direct an awakened ethical conscience, but provide no regular ("routinized") approach to intense religious experience oriented toward cosmic goals. Among liberal Jews we see a Mosaic ethic and "peoplehood" without Mosaic law or community life; among liberal Protestants, a gospel of charity without dramatic communication with Jesus.

So while the "religiously musical" are born into most communities, the liberal traditions serve other purposes than to offer the virtuoso a full-bodied mythic score he can interpret or to provide routinized methods for the spiritually less gifted who would still like to practice. Such resources are available, however, along with spiritual masters, in the conservative traditions of the West—for those who are willing to pay the price. The initial price for access to the spiritual masters who still do exist in Catholic monasticism and Hasidic tradition is a radical break with the secular world: withdrawal to a monastery or acceptance of the full yoke of Mosaic law. As we have seen, evangelistic Protestants ideally function as hortatory preachers, not spiritual masters with a method; charismatic Christianity, moreover, works through "spontaneous" conversion—admittedly granted only to a few—and generally necessitates an initial confrontation with a radically exclusive and nonscientific fundamentalist doctrine.

For many Westerners brought up with secular presuppositions, such costs may be excessive—especially when demanded in advance, without a prior sample of the goods. So it is not surprising that Indian holy men presenting a unifying (if not entirely undogmatic) teaching, together with some accessible, methodical practice, can find a Western audience—particularly, in the United States, among those from liberal Protestant and Reform Jewish backgrounds.[22] They fulfill a demand among a specific constituency of the "religiously musical" to which Western tradition does not at present cater.

As holy men, the Indian gurus frequently have an attitude toward theological issues that emphasizes pragmatism over consistency—a most viable approach for teaching skeptical Westerners. True, the teaching they espouse normally demands a coming to terms with an alien religio-philosophical tradition, but this tradition uses an idiom of natural substance that often appears to accommodate the truths of Western science in ways less strained than those commonly found in Western theology. The traditional approach of Indian gurus to yogic practice has also been pragmatic, if somewhat authoritarian ("Do it and you'll see"), so spiritual practices can with some legitimacy be presented to Westerners (and Westernized Indians) as techniques that, when applied methodically, yield "empiric" results. The guru can thus even find a basis in his tradition for dealing with Westerners who approach him as if for "spiritual music lessons," and may eventually inspire in some a more respectful—if not adoring—style of Indian guru-devotion.

Most often the techniques these gurus offer derive from traditional yogic practices of an esoteric nature, but taken down to basics for crowds of beginners, and shorn of elaborate ritual elements for consumption in the West. Now it is just this combination of esoteric power and popular simplicity that is characteristic of practices long espoused in the Indian environment by the Hindi sants, who drew on a tradition originating in an age of newly apparent religious plurality and cultural stress that bears comparison with our own.

Certainly, of all the various modern inheritors of the medieval sant tradition, it is no doubt members of sant *panths* who serve the low Indian sociological strata closest to those in which the early sants typically moved: the Radhasoamis emerged in the nineteenth century, after sant tradition had become respectable among the middle castes. But when Radhasoami gurus today offer an uncomplicated, effective practice claimed to lie at the root of all religions, they can be seen as reviving the role of the early sants—unifying holy men in a pluralistic socio-historic context—if among other classes and in a shrunken world. And it is those Radhasoami gurus that do indeed function in this way—most notably those of the extended Beas sublineage—who have gained significant followings in the West. Finding sources in an established tradition originally developed to be accessible to large numbers beyond the Hindu pale, these sants—alongside some others from the Marāṭhī tradition[23]—have functioned naturally among Westerners while still remaining close to their spiritual roots at home. If they thrive in the West it may be because the fruits of Indian spiritual culture they offer are at once robustly genuine and better suited to Western tastes than many others. For the average Western spiritual consumer will not easily digest strange and complex myths and rituals—found in most Indian religion but typically disdained by the sants. Thus, while sant piety still presents fruits that seem exotic for the Western market, these nevertheless meet a demand within it—and are none the less sweet for being available.

NOTES

/1/ Hacking's experience is described in the Introduction, p. 6.
/2/ The classic exposition of the Bloomfieldian approach is Leonard Bloomfield, *Language* (New York: Holt, Rinehart, and Winston, 1933).
/3/ On strong and weak universals see David McNeill, "Are There Specifically Linguistic Universals?" in *Semantics*, ed. Danny D. Steinberg and Leon A. Jakobovits (Cambridge: Cambridge University Press, 1971), pp. 530–535.
/4/ An overview of some of the earlier research on language universals is provided by Charles A. Ferguson in "Historical Background of Universals Research" in *Universals of Human Language, vol. 1: Method and Theory,* ed. Joseph Greenberg (Stanford: Stanford University Press, 1978), pp. 7–32.
/5/ The most elegant explanation of this sort is proposed by Theo Vennemann, who reduces to the single relation of operator/operand all the following syntactic relationships:

operator	operand
object	verb
adjective	noun
genitive	noun
relative clause	noun
noun phrase	adposition
standard of comparison	comparative adjective

Most languages then show a definite tendency toward *either* operator/operand word order *or* operand/operator. The tabular presentation of Vennemann's categories is from Bernard Comrie, *Language Universals and Linguistic Typology* (Chicago: University of Chicago Press, 1981), p. 92; there Vennemann's argument is presented in a discussion of generalizations from Greenberg's statistical results (pp. 89–96). Vennemann presents the argument himself in "Analogy in Generative Grammar: The Origin of Word Order" in *Proceedings of the Eleventh International Congress of Linguistics*, ed. Luigi Heilmann (Bologna: Societa Editrice il Mulino, 1972) 2:79–83. He draws on the work of Lehmann; see *Syntactic Typology: Studies in the Phenomenology of Language*, ed. Winfred P. Lehmann (Austin: University of Texas Press, 1978).
/6/ On the characteristics of structuralist explanations see Philip Pettit, *The Concept of Structuralism: A Critical Analysis* (Berkeley: University of California Press, 1975).

/7/ See Ino Rossi, "Intellectual Antecedents of Lévi-Strauss' Notion of Unconscious" in *The Unconscious in Culture: The Structuralism of Claude Lévi-Strauss in Perspective* (New York: Dutton, 1974), pp. 14–16.
/8/ On the historical significance of the program of universal linguists see Neil Smith and Deirdre Wilson, *Modern Linguistics: The Results of Chomsky's Revolution* (Harmondsworth: Penguin, 1979), p. 9.
/9/ On the development of traditional Indian law see Robert Lingat, *The Classical Law of India*, trans. J. Duncan M. Derrett (Berkeley: University of California Press, 1973).
/10/ In *Joseph Karo: Lawyer and Mystic* (Oxford: Oxford University Press, 1962), R. J. Zwi Werblowsky reveals the important place of mystical experience in the life of one of medieval Judaism's most important legists; he treats the mystical life of the Vilna *gaon*, pp. 311–16.
/11/ Gershom Scholem tells us of "the feebleness of [the] image of the Messiah" in Lurianic Kabbalah (*Sabbatai Ṣevi*, trans. R. J. Zwi Werblowsky [Princeton: Princeton University Press, 1973], pp. 52–59).
/12/ In nineteenth-century Russia, for example, Seraphim of Sarov and Father Ambrose of Optino were famous for attracting large numbers of lay people, sometimes from the elite classes. See Sergius Bolshakoff, *Russian Mystics* (Kalamazoo: Cistercian Publishing Co., 1976), pp. 122–44, 187–90.
/13/ See Roland H. Bainton, *Erasmus of Christendom* (London: Fontana), pp. 209–211.
/14/ On the role of Western missionaries in the discovery of Kabīr, see Charlotte Vaudeville, *Kabīr*, pp. 11–17.
/15/ The terms are used in Weber, "The Social Psychology of the World Religions" in *From Max Weber: Essays in Sociology*, trans. and ed. H[ans] H. Gerth and C. Wright Mills (New York: Oxford University Press, 1958), pp. 287–288.
/16/ Stanley Jeyaraja Tambiah, *The Buddhist Saints of the Forest and the Cult of Amulets* (Cambridge: Cambridge University Press, 1984), pp. 321–334, gives a reappraisal of Weberian types in the Indic context.
/17/ Frank E. Reynolds and Regina T. Clifford discuss the symbiosis between the *sangha* and the laity in Thailand: "Sangha, Society and the Struggle for National Liberation in Thailand" in *Transitions and Transformations in the History of Religions*, ed. Frank E. Reynolds and Theodore M. Ludwig (Leiden: E. J. Brill, 1980). Tambiah, *Saints of the Forest*, presents the role of modern Thai meditation masters. Richard F. Gombrich, *Precept and Practice* (Oxford: Clarendon Press, 1971), pp. 284–293, describes beliefs about the coming of Maitreya in Ceylon.
/18/ Mircea Eliade, *Patterns in Comparative Religion* (New York: Meridien, 1963), pp. 45–50.
/19/ Religious rationalization is discussed by Weber in "Social Psychology," pp. 283–294.
/20/ On the emergence of the sants in pre-Mughal India see my *Lord as Guru*, pp. 207–210.
/21/ Milton B. Singer, "The Radha-Krishna Bhajanas of Madras City," offers a classic study on urban devotion in modern South India (in his *When a Great Tradition Modernizes* [New York: Praeger, 1972]).
/22/ J. Stillson Judah, *Hare Krishna and the Counterculture* (New York:

John Wiley and Sons, 1974), p. 147, gives some statistics on the family affiliation of members of the Hare Krishna movement. 29.5% came out of large, liberal Protestant denominations; 14.5% (out of a total national population of 3%) were Jewish, 18% were Catholic and a few came from small, unorthodox Christian groups. A full 32% listed their previous affiliation as "none" or "other." Most remarkable, the largest Protestant denomination in America, the conservative Southern Baptists, are not represented, nor are evangelicals. See also Harvey Cox, *Turning East* (New York: Simon and Schuster, 1977), pp. 94–95.

/23/ On Swami Muktananda, in the Marāṭhī tradition, see Charles S. J. White "Swami Muktananda and the Enlightenment through Śakti-Pāt" *History of Religions* 13:306–322.

EPILOGUE:

REALITY AND IMAGINATION AMONG RELIGIONISTS AND SANTS

Sects and teachers offering a new religious identity are not the only vehicles through which the fruits of exotic pieties have been brought to the West; access to non-Western myths and doctrines has also been offered by some scholars—particularly those in the humanities who write about religious traditions. Packaging their goods in ways that reflect the alternative realities distinguished at the outset of this book, religious teachers and scholarly interpreters aim at different markets. Yet like devotees, scholars, too, are fascinated by the mysteries they see in non-Western traditions, and in attempting to comprehend them seem to draw on similar sources of imagination. Thus grounded in similar sources of imagination but different senses of reality, the practices of devotees and religionists are likely to present both curious parallels and interesting contrasts.

To both scholars and devotees, the imaginative creations of religious traditions are objects to be taken seriously. Devotees, recognizing particular images of the divine as links to ultimate reality, attempt to appropriate them personally and completely. Scholars, immediately concerned with a reality less ultimate, attempt to comprehend the religious objects less completely as well as less personally. Yet at the same time, the very distance demanded by academic study may lay open depths of the religious imagination previously closed to us, giving us access to symbolic complexities at which personal Western monotheistic sensibilities might shrink. Comprehending unwieldy ritual and abstruse doctrine in our own terms, as scholars we realize common human meanings in myth, image, and dogma that we could approach in no other way. To those of us committed to a version of Western rationalism, the academic study of religion may offer the only avenue available to some of the more exuberant profundities of the religious imagination—seen on a vaster scale than that offered by any one non-Western tradition, if less deeply.

Encountering the same materials as those known to devotees, we may also have similar problems in comprehending them. It makes sense, then, to look to some of the dynamics of religious traditions in pondering problems of our own tradition of scholarship. Do the resemblances we find among disparate materials sometimes strike us as similar to those of Kabbalistic speculation? Do our attempts at editing and footnoting recall those of ancient Chinese scholars, who often liked to rummage in ancient sources to cull support for their interpretations?[1] I do not suggest that we take religious traditions as models, but instead, that we learn from their difficulties. Perhaps our critical distance can help us resolve problems to which both religious traditions and religious studies are liable. Certainly, the diversity of the traditions we study contributes to the complexity of the problems we face; but each tradition may also give us a perspective on our own scholarly endeavor.

The example of the sants might elucidate some problems of individuals and tradition in the history of religions, of collective identity and cumulative knowledge. Like many sants, historians of religion are familiar with more than one orthodox religion but are likely to be skeptical of the absolute truth of any. Emerging, like the sants in pre-Mughal India, during an epoch undergoing the impact of cultures, we are like them masters of synthesis, constructing the worlds we know out of pieces of several. And since our visions are thus so distinct among themselves, like the sants we have problems recognizing our community. At the broadest level, are we, like the sants, just a vaguely related clan—sharing some peculiar attitudes toward the stuff of religion but not much more? Certainly, within our broad clan we seem, like the sants, to have a few identifiable lineages of gurus and disciples, as well as institutional centers to which adherents occasionally make pilgrimage. Such structure as we have in our traditions, moreover, has at times developed in directions all too familiar from the sant *paths*.

Indeed, some of the focal points we have found in our search for collective identity seem to resemble the immanent foci seen at the root of religious communities. Our revered gurus of the past, often unique individuals with an unorthodox, all-encompassing perspective, appear transformed into singular personalities. Figures like Van der Leeuw and Eliade, though never quite worshipped, have sometimes been taken, like Lord Rām, to offer inviolable archetypal models. Yet the diverse intuitions we bring to scholarship on religions seem to tolerate no single set of archetypes, no one way of doing things that can satisfy us all. Some of us, then, have gone to the other extreme. Having understood that no great personality can offer the single true way for history of religions, we have divorced ourselves from all personalities, including our own. From this perspective, our task is to practice history and philology only, careful to observe the fine points of our scholarly heritage. Mastering the techniques through which our knowledge may be captured in its pristine state, we manipulate and add to a cumulative tradition of recorded facts, references, and footnotes. By taking care of the minutiae fostered by our academic heritage, we will eventually come to the only truths we can know. In this guise, we resemble scholarly brahmins, who have done their duty if they are punctilious in the observance of the necessary rituals and construe their texts properly.

The ends to which either of these directions can lead, alas, are all too visible from the sant *panths*. Those of us revering a great personality appear to those outside as the members of a cult, forbidding and inaccessible; tight disciplinary coherence is gained at the expense of members' numbers and individual creativity. A concern with the sources of knowledge divorced from any distinctive personal vision, on the other hand, may lead us to total absorption into an anonymous scholarly heritage, as individuals following conventional rules but leaving no memorable insights. The major lesson from this analogy may be that the best way for history of religions to avoid the fate of a withering sectarian institution is to avoid any dogmas of its own. Thus, continuing to use intuitions sparked by contact with religious materials, we must not forget the tentative nature of religio-historical realities. These are partial realities, not ultimate ones; pieces of truth, not complete doctrines. None is final, but they all may offer temporary insight.

Giving us a critical distance from our own and others' imaginative constructs, an awareness of the partial, tentative truths with which we deal also gives us the freedom to build on them. Iconoclasm, as we are reminded by the sants' Formless Lord, is in its origins a religious term, one grounded in the conviction that ultimate reality lies beyond the world of forms. But it is in this human world of forms that the truths we seek to understand are located, in men and women struggling to use their inherited traditions to come to grips with their situations in the universe they know. The entities we posit to describe these human situations appear believable just to the extent that we *can* build on them, using them to hold together a connected body of religio-historical knowledge. None of what we tentatively construct is eternal, and much will not last long at all. But this early stage in the growth of our collective knowledge seems to call for tolerance as well as experimentation. If we cannot examine the reality of others' religio-historical constructs by using them ourselves, let us at least take the trouble to see their significance in the world in which they are described. Unbridled critical iconoclasm is likely to leave us with little indeed: no body of relative knowledge and no Formless Lord either.

A body of cumulative knowledge that explores some commonalities of the human religious condition, one that is aware of its imaginative roots, is built around shared concepts, and grows through critical assent: is this a chimera only, the vision of a field that can never exist? Perhaps. But if it is an hallucination, where does it come from? And whence arise all the other diverse visions of history of religions lurking in the minds of scholars? Does not the idea of history of religions give some practitioners in the field a sense of identity in their world that a concept of sant tradition gives to some religious practitioners in theirs? However idiosyncratic we may be in our world views and the traditions we know, a belief in history of religions assures us that we are not just individuals alone in the scholarly desert, but are part of a definite, larger whole. Though we work with our own, often highly specific, materials, the dimensions of our research are potentially infinite; and though the field in fact seems infinitely diffuse, it in fact has at least a few specific dimensions. Presenting the same potentially religious complementarity of infinite and specific that we have seen in the idea of sant tradition, the idea of history of religions may stem from much the same place. And it may be just as real.

NOTE

/1/ Catherine Bell has made some provocative remarks about the practices of Chinese editors in "Charisma and Classification: Chinese Morality Books," a paper read at the 1986 conference the American Academy of Religions.

BASIC BIBLIOGRAPHY

1. Theory

Brewer, Marilynn B. and Barry E. Collins eds. *Scientific Inquiry and the Social Sciences: A Volume in Honor of Donald T. Campbell*. San Francisco: Jossey-Bass Publishers, 1981.

Comrie, Bernard. *Language Universals and Linguistic Typology*. Chicago: University of Chicago Press, 1981.

Eliade, Mircea. *Patterns in Comparative Religion*. New York: Meridien, 1963.

Geertz, Clifford C. *The Interpretation of Cultures*. New York: Basic Books, 1973.

Greenberg, Joseph, ed. *Universals of Human Language, vol. 1: Method and Theory*. Stanford: Stanford University Press, 1978.

Hacking, Ian. *Representing and Intervening: Introductory Topics in the Philosophy of Natural Science*. Cambridge: Cambridge University Press, 1983.

Kuhn, Thomas S. "The Essential Tension: Tradition and Innovation in Scientific Research." In *The Essential Tension: Selected Studies in Scientific Tradition and Change*. Chicago: University of Chicago Press, 1977. Pp. 223–239.

Lakatos, Imre and Alan Musgrave, eds. *Criticism and the Growth of Knowledge*. London: Cambridge University Press, 1970.

Lehmann, Winfred, ed. *Syntactic Typology: Studies in the Phenomenology of Language*. Austin: University of Texas Press, 1978.

Pettit, Philip. *The Concept of Structuralism: A Critical Analysis*. Berkeley: University of California Press, 1975.

Smith, Neil and Deirdre Wilson. *Modern Linguistics: The Results of Chomsky's Revolution*. Harmondsworth: Penguin, 1979.

Turner, Victor. *The Forest of Symbols: Aspects of Ndembu Ritual*. Ithaca and London: Cornell University Press, 1967.

Vennemann, Theo. "Analogy in Generative Grammar: The Origin of Word Order." In *Proceedings of the Eleventh International Con-*

gress of Linguistics, ed. Luigi Heilmann. Bologna: Societa Editrice il Mulino, 1972. Vol. 2, pp. 79–83.

Weber, Max. *Sociology of Religion*, trans. Ephraim Fischoff. Boston: Beacon Press, 1964.

———. "The Social Psychology of the World Religions." In *From Max Weber: Essays in Sociology*, trans. and ed. H[ans] H. Gerth and C. Wright Mills. New York: Oxford University Press, 1958. Pp. 287–88.

Wimsatt, William C. "Robustness, Reliability, and Overdetermination." In Brewer and Collins. Pp. 124–163.

2. The Sants in India

Bakker, Hans. *Ayodhyā*. Groningen Oriental Studies, vol. 1. Groningen: Egbert Forsten, 1986.

Caturvedī, Pāraśurām. *Uttarī Bhārat kī Sant Paramparā*, 3rd ed. Allahabad: Leader Press, 1972.

Gold, Daniel. *The Lord as Guru: Hindi Sants in North Indian Tradition*. New York: Oxford University Press, 1987.

———. "Clan and Lineage among the Sants." In Schomer and McLeod. Pp. 305–327.

Gold, Daniel and Ann Grodzins Gold. "The Fate of the Householder Nath." *History of Relgions* 24:113–32 (Nov. 1984).

Govind Sāhib. *Govind Sudhā*. Govind Sāhib, Faizābād: Mahant Śrī Rām Komal Dās Sāheb, 1976.

Inden, Ronald and Ralph Nicholas. *Kinship in Bengali Culture*. Chicago: University of Chicago Press, 1977.

Mathur, Agam Prasad. *Radhasoami Faith*. Delhi: Vikas, 1974.

Palṭū Sāhib. *Palṭū Darśan*. Ayodhyā: Śrīmān Mahant Rāmsumer Dāsjī Maharāj, 1977.

———. *Palṭū Sāhib kī Bānī*, 3 vols. Allahabad: Belvedere Press, 1965–67.

———. *Śri Palṭū Sāhib krit Śabdāvalī*. Ayodhyā: Mahant Jagannāth Dās Jī Maharāj, 1950.

Prabhū Dās, *Govind Sāhab kā Sankṣipt Itihās*. Govind Sāhib, Faizābād: Mahant Śrī Rām Komal Dās Sāheb, 1976.

Puri, Lekh Raj. *Radha Swami Teachings*, 2nd ed. Beas, Punjab: Radhasoami Satsang, 1972.

Robinson, James B. *Buddha's Lions: The Lives of the Eighty-Four Siddhas*. Berkeley: Dharma Publishing, 1979.

Schomer, Karine and W. H. McLeod, eds. *The Sants: Studies in a Devotional Tradition of India*. Berkeley: Graduate Theological Union, Berkeley Religious Studies Series and Delhi: Motilal Banarsi Dass, 1987.

Shukla, Bhagvatī Prasād. *Bavarī-Panth ke Hindī-Kavi*. New Delhi: Arya Book Depot, 1972.

Singh, Rādhā Krishna. *Sant Palṭū Dās aur Palṭū Panth*. New Delhi: Sūrya Prakāśan, 1966.

Vaudeville, Charlotte. *Kabīr*. Oxford: Oxford University Press, 1974.